The Art of Digital Persuasion

Jeff Hasen

Copyright © 2019 Jeff Hasen

All rights reserved.

ISBN: 9781796593624

Dedication

This book is dedicated to Kathryn, my wife and partner, who brings sunshine even on dreary Seattle days and who has had me looking forward to Date Night for 1,456 consecutive weeks and counting.

Table of Contents

Introduction		vii
Chapter One	The Insatiable Mobile Appetite	1
Chapter Two	For Gen Z, Mobile Is The New Primetime	6
Chapter Three	The Digital Universe	10
Chapter Four	New Technology	15
Chapter Five	How ESPN Tackles Other Screens and Interfaces	28
Chapter Six	Neiman Marcus: A Century-Plus of Retail Innovation	33
Chapter Seven	Personalization: Catering To An Audience of One	40
Chapter Eight	Expedia: Traveling Into the Future	50
Chapter Nine	Twitter: Creating Emotional Connections	59
Chapter Ten	Amazon: Giving Your Brand A Voice	66
Chapter Eleven	Microsoft: The Recipe To Get Mixed Results	74
Chapter Twelve	How To View Innovation	80
Chapter Thirteen	The New Breed of Marketer	88
Chapter Fourteen	Mobile's Role Moving Forward	96
Chapter Fifteen	Even More Innovation	109

Conclusion	115
Acknowledgements	121
The Experts	123
The Author	131

Introduction

The Most Personal Relationship
In 2015, I wrote *The Art of Mobile Persuasion*, a book about the relationships that people have with their mobile devices.

It's safe to describe them then and now as intimate, engrossing and integral.

The central questions in *The Art of Mobile Persuasion* were whether brands have opportunities to get in on that action or is three a crowd?

Since then, some businesses have muffed the chance, taking an approach that has been deemed as invasive, impersonal, and/or offering no value. But others large and small have knocked gently, ingratiated themselves, brought something that was welcomed, and seen resulting increases in awareness, loyalty and sales.

To the former group, what were you thinking? Or, at the risk of hurling an insult right out of the chute, were you?

To the latter, we're good now, right?

Well, no.

Why? The playing field has changed.

New Suitors Have Come-A-Knockin'
Our nurtured customers and prospects are now being wooed by other means.

Though voice interfaces.

And wearables.

Smart appliances, even toilets (life is complete when you are wooed by a biffy. Am I right?)

And OTT (over the top) devices.

Virtual and mixed reality software and hardware.

And the list goes on. There's every reason to believe that the pulls for attention will grow this year, next year, and every year after that.

Of course, this brings with it all sorts of complications.

- Where will we find our customers and prospects?
- Where we do want to lead them and what must they find when they get there?
- How does all of this innovation affect the customer journey?
- If personalization is the so-called North Star, how do we deliver this on the screens and interfaces of today – and the ones surely coming behind those?

And how does the relationship that your brand has steadily built with customers via the mobile phone survive, evolve, and thrive when eyes and ears are drawn to even more places?

Expanding The View of The Landscape

For *The Art of Digital Persuasion,* the conversation broadens to today's interfaces, devices, behaviors and technologies.

I again have had the pleasure and privilege of visiting with some of the sharpest marketers and other business leaders that one can identify. I sought out real-world experience, perspective, and advice to give us the knowledge, skills and confidence that we all need to do our jobs — and, in many cases, to reimagine our current outdated positions given these upended times.

We'll share what leaders from Amazon, Google, Microsoft, Twitter, ESPN, and others are doing and thinking to address the core question of this book:

Now what?

"Our mission statement is the exact same as it was when the company was founded (in 1979)," ESPN's Ryan Spoon, Senior Vice President of Digital and Social, told me. "And it is to serve sports fans, anytime, anywhere. The definition of anywhere and that expectation from the fans is the thing that has changed."

I went back to Google's Jason Spero, a powerful voice in *The Art of Mobile Persuasion*, to provide an updated roadmap for marketers given the proliferation of new stuff.

"The consumer doesn't see the technology, " the Vice President, Performance Media, explained to me. "What the consumer sees is that they should be able to continue their game from a tablet to a mobile phone. That is a logical, rational, human thought. And so the better we can do in our research of studying those expectations of consumers, of understanding the moments where they expect things of us, and then drag the technology along with us kicking and screaming, we need to build those experiences.

"It's likely the question of when we get to the finish line might be the wrong metaphor. But rather how do we recognize those consumers' expectations and how might we be able to serve her needs in a way where she may not see the technology but she's delighted by the experience?"

We Are Still Attempting To Persuade
The brand marketer's interest in persuading hasn't changed although we will hear from one leader who contends that it's all about identifying and fulfilling needs rather than changing someone's mind.

What is not in dispute is the fact that our roles have become more complex. And our playbooks must change again.

"This wouldn't be a job if it was easy," said Scott Emmons, the longtime innovation lab lead at retailer Neiman Marcus.

We'll examine the characteristics of winners and hone in on the importance of having what Microsoft CEO Satya Nadella and others call a growth mindset.

We'll demystify such terms as machine learning and artificial intelligence and provide actionable steps for you to be more data-driven.

We'll go all in on the new interfaces and bring expert opinion on how and when to consider bringing each into your marketing mix.

"We don't have 10 years to figure it out," global marketer Tamara McCleary told me, citing the increased pressure on us to move from business cost to revenue driver. "We've got 10 minutes."

OK, the clock is ticking. Let's go.

We'll begin as we did in 2015 — by getting us all on a level playing field.

Chapter One

The Insatiable Mobile Appetite

All You Can Eat

When it comes to mobile, by now, you've heard it all, so much so that these statements seem like clichés.

The mobile phone is the remote control for life.

Most sleep with their mobile phone within four feet away.

People would rather give up sex than their device.

More people on Earth have a mobile phone than a toothbrush or a toilet.

There is no place that is a device-free zone, including the potty.

Do you know what?

They are all true.

By The Numbers

By 2018, wireless penetration in the United States had exceeded 100 percent, meaning that there was more than one mobile phone for every person from coast to coast. That's not new. In fact, it has been the case for a half-decade.[1]

What had changed was the adoption of the smartphone. Through 2017, Americans were enthralled with 273 million of those, compared to "only" 109 million in 2000, according to CTIA, a wireless trade association.

The cellphone had changed the way we communicate (or don't communicate), buy, share, deposit a check, and gauge our health, among tens of other things that will never be the same.

In developing countries, the mobile phone literally was a lifeline, leading to cleaner water, more diagnosis and treatment of disease, and upticks in banking for the unbanked.

There were now more than 5.1 billion global wireless users (CTIA).

I'll lay it out in even more numbers, but as I wrote in *The Art of Mobile Persuasion,* I advise you to view these statistics as directional and as a point in time. Mobile morphs that fast.

Mobile Users Are Attracted To Their Screens

Americans averaged 3.3 hours a day on mobile device, meaning more than half of the 5.9 hours in digital media were with a cellphone (analyst Mary Meeker).[2]

---

[1] CTIA: https://www.ctia.org/the-wireless-industry/infographics-library: Feb. 2019

[2] Mary Meeker: http://info.localytics.com/blog/heres-what-mobile-teams-need-to-know-from-mary-meekers-2018-internet-trends-deck): June 18, 2018

Eighty-five percent of photos taken in 2017 were captured on a smartphone (CTIA).

Fifty-four percent of e-book readers used their phone to read (CTIA).

We had seen 330 percent growth in health & fitness apps over the last three years (CTIA).

Seventy-six percent of travelers said that a mobile phone was the most important trip accessory (CTIA).

Eighty-nine percent always had their mobile device within arm's reach (CTIA).

My choice for *oh, my gosh* factoid?

Being close to good schools was no longer the top reason that consumers cited when they were picking a new place to live (CTIA).

Two-thirds said that wireless coverage was number one on the list. Good schools followed at 65 percent. After that came affordable house at 60 percent and commuting time at 41 percent.

Mobile is *that* important to us.

Sizing It Up

This all means what?

In the United States, at least, dismiss the malarkey around "mobile only." The small screen is the dominant screen so, if you are like most, at the very least it has to be considered in your marketing toolbox. Forgetting that, or worse, failing to act upon it, will put you and your enterprise behind or even out of business.

Four years ago, Forrester's Julie Ask told us that 62 percent of marketers still treated devices as just smaller PCs. More damning was the fact that 89 percent of companies had a mobile strategy to have consumers come to them. Of course, that was all wrong. Consumers expect brands to engage with them where *they* are.

And, as you will see in this book, our customers and prospects are in more places. And their expectations grow every year.

For now, I'll point you to two views about where we are with mobile.

"We've made enormous progress understanding consumer behavior and understanding the relationship between the digital world and the physical world," Google's Jason Spero told me. "Consumers use both."

"We used to talk about the mobile user and the desktop user. Now we know that we have one user with one journey and we start to understand the interplay between that user's many different touchpoints and the brand. We have a better understanding from a data standpoint and a conceptual standpoint. At the individual marketer level, some are doing a better job. Some have really built holistic models in terms of the value of the engagement and the role of the different touchpoints."

Gartner research director Noah Elkin, who like Spero has been in mobile for so long that he is considered a lifer, shared what he sees as specific areas of progress.

"We think in a more sophisticated way about how mobile functions across the customer journey," he told me.

"Not just as a separate channel and sometimes as an add-on, but how it can play a starring or supporting role at different stages."

For example, he pointed to wireless being the optimal avenue to reach consumers in context, meaning at the right place and time.

"Mobile plays this key function as the remote control for the whole experience," he said.

What many still fail to get is in the area of expectations. Users have no patience for mediocre or bad experiences and often vote by taking their attention and wallet elsewhere.

"In some places, I feel encouraged that we are building what the consumer wants from us," Google's Spero said, "but in most cases I would say during that time that we were catching up, I feel that we are still chasing consumer expectations. Consumers expect certain things to work and expect things from us.

"Whoever you are, wherever category you are in, consumers don't just compare you to your competition. So if you're Toyota, they just don't compare you to Nissan. They want the experience they have when they engage with you on a mobile device to be the best experience that they've ever had. If they are getting a better experience from Airbnb or Lyft, we need to continue to try to build for that and we've got some work to do."

That work includes getting current on usage and penetration of the Web and social media. But first, let's spend a bit more time looking at how mobile has impacted generational behavior.

Chapter Two

For Gen Z, Mobile Is The New Primetime

The Preferred Screen
To misunderstand today's youth is to view their digital habits as some sort of a tectonic shift.

Away from the television set.

Away from mass programming.

Away from long-established viewing dayparts.

For that to be true, Generation Z would have had to had started with large screens, habits of watching shows from the big networks, and a regimen of primarily engaging with content during the evening hours.

None of that, in fact, is reality.

Some of those born between 1998 and 2016 undoubtedly had a mobile phone in one hand with a pacifier in the others. We, ummm, had an Etch A Sketch (hey there, my young reader, Google it).

Preferred screen?

While you and I can point to our very own first television as a milestone moment, Gen Z considers getting a phone as an important life event. Today's teens got their first phone when they were around 12.

Desired content?

Seven in 10 teens told Google that they spent more than three hours per day watching mobile video. And much of the consumption came via YouTube, Snapchat and Instagram, and was user generated rather than Hollywood produced.

Time of day?

The smartphone is in Gen Z's hands from sun up well past dinner time. Viewing happens on the bus, at the lunch table, during recess, and every other time that this group wants to be entertained, informed or otherwise occupied.

For Gen Z, mobile is the new primetime.

While *Fast Company* wrote that "media and market research companies have labeled Generation Z 'screen addicts' with the attention span of a gnat," ignoring the generation's influence on a company's business success is a foolish exercise for a marketer.

Gen Z was 26 percent of the U.S. population with $44 billion annual purchasing power. Two in three teens made purchases online and, of those, more than half were making purchases on their phones.

But capturing their attention is not without challenges. Gen Z was 80 percent more likely to always be multi-screening compared to their parents, per Tremor Media and Hulu.

Here's more from an excellent series of reports by Google:

"Gen Z never knew the world before the Internet — before everything you could ever need was one click away. They never knew the world before terrorism or global warming. As a result, Gen Z is the most informed, evolved, and empathetic generation of its kind. They value information, stimulation, and connection, evident by their affinity for YouTube, Google, and Netflix.

"They also have high hopes for the brands they choose. From Nike to Xbox, they expect big things. As professionals, we should see this as our challenge to live up to the standard Gen Z has set for us and to continue to inform, inspire, and create products and marketing that facilitate the world in which they want to live."

Of course, not all Gen Z'ers are the same. It's prudent for marketers to understand the nuances.

For black teens, mobile music rules.

Eighty-six percent did so on their phones every week, significantly more than all teens, and nearly 6 in 10 said they spent more than three hours every day listening to music on their phones.

Two in three black teens made purchases online, and of those, more than half were making purchases on their phones.

Black teens were more likely to have positive attitudes towards brands, and to consider them "cool" if they felt as though the message is personalized to them.

Nearly one-quarter of all 13-to-17-year-olds were Hispanic, and they were the fastest-growing teen demographic.

While listening to music was the top mobile activity, 3 in 4 Hispanic teens said they spent 3+ hours per day watching videos on their phones.

Eight in 10 Hispanic teens made purchases online, compared to two-thirds of all teens. And of those who shop online, over half were making most of their purchases on their phones.

As to advertising, Gen Z'ers actually aren't unique in their thinking.

For teens, ads impact a product's "cool" factor. What makes a product cool?

- If my friends are talking about it
- If I see an ad about it
- If it's something personalized to me

But when it comes to social media, Gen Z was two to three times more likely to be influenced by social media than by sales or discounts — the only generation to value social media over price when it comes to making purchase decisions, according to a study by IRI.

And Gen Z was twice as likely to convert on mobile.

The upshot for marketers?

At the least, we are in need of a mental shift that causes us to look at today in an entirely new way. Just as Gen Z is doing.

Chapter Three

The Digital Universe

Assessing The Landscape and Digital's Place
Long gone for most are the days of dismal dial-up Internet connections and flip phones that forced triple-tapping to construct accurate messages. Changes have occurred led by the tsunami-like adoption of smartphones. However, it's a colossal mistake to believe that our digital lives are now locked into place.

Let's review some data to get a sense of who was doing what through 2018:

The number of global Internet users reached 4.021 billion, up seven percent year-over-year. Much of that growth came from outside North America in places including Africa (We Are Social).[3]

Nearly 280 million people, or 85 percent of the U.S. population, were projected to be online at least once a month in 2018, according to eMarketer. Digital video viewing remained the most popular digital media activity with 82 percent watching this type of content regularly. Digital

---
3 We Are Social: Jan. 30, 2018

audio listening and social networking were at 72 percent and 71 percent of Internet users, respectfully. Digital gaming was at 58 percent of Internet users (We Are Social).

Digging Deeper on Social Media
The number of social media users grew to 3.2 billion worldwide, up 13 percent year-over-year. This came despite repeated data breaches of large social networks and the introduction of usage monitoring tools that some sought out as a way to reach a "healthier" balance between off-line and on-line activities (more on that later).

Around two-thirds (68 percent) of U.S. adults used Facebook, the most popular social network (Pew).[4]

Among U.S. adults who used Facebook, 74 percent visited the site at least once a day. Facebook remained popular among all demographic groups. Seventy-four percent of women in the U.S. used the platform, compared with 62 percent of men.

Eighty-one percent of those ages 18 to 29 used Facebook — about twice the share among those 65 and older (41 percent). However, the share of older Americans who used the platform had doubled since August 2012, when just 20 percent of those 65 and older said they used it.

Facebook was being used by around half of America's teens, but it no longer dominated the teen social media landscape. By 2018, 51 percent of those ages 13 to 17

---
4 Pew: http://www.pewresearch.org/fact-tank/2018/10/24/facts-about-americans-and-facebook/: Feb. 1, 2019

said they used the platform, down from 71 percent in a 2014-2015 survey.

Looking Beyond Facebook

Nearly 168 million in the U.S. were monthly users of Instagram (Statista).[5] About 111 million used Facebook Messenger, followed by Twitter at just over 70 million, and Pinterest at slightly more than 52 million. WhatsApp, the most used messaging app worldwide, had nearly 21 million U.S. users.

Roughly eight-in-ten teens ages 13 to 17 said to Pew[6] that social media made them feel more connected to what was going on in their friends' lives, while around two-thirds said these platforms made them feel as if they had people who will support them through tough times.

About 60 percent of teens said that they spent time with their friends online on a daily or nearly daily basis. Some 45 percent of teens said they felt overwhelmed by all the drama on social media, with 13 percent saying they felt this way "a lot."

A similar share of teens (44 percent) said they often or sometimes unfriended or unfollowed others on social media. When asked why they had digitally disconnected from others, 78 percent of this group reported doing so because people created too much drama, while 52 percent cited the bullying of them or others.

---

5 Statista: https://www.statista.com/topics/1882/instagram/: 2019
6 Pew: http://www.pewresearch.org/fact-tank/2019/02/01/facts-about-americans-and-facebook/: Feb. 1, 2019

Digital's Influence in Omnichannel Retail

When it came to retail, despite the headlines about the woes suffered by physical stores, the great majority of shopping was still done offline. Sure, online was quickly taking share, but it was also playing an important complementary role with traditional shopping.

Consider:

A study by the Harvard Business Review[7] found that 73 percent could be described as "omnichannellers" — buying across any one store's digital and physical channels.

Millennials were highly invested in shopping through digital channels now and in the future, as 87 percent[8] said that they would be more likely to shop at a retailer that was digitally innovative (Salmon).

More than 65 percent of consumers conducted online product research before setting foot in a store, amplifying the need for retailers to optimize digital experiences[9] (Retail Dive).

It wasn't enough just to have something for customers to see in-store. The bar had been raised as evidenced by the fact that nine out of ten retailers were planning to

---

7 Harvard Business Review: https://www.fourthsource.com/loyalty/technology-re-defining-traditional-retail-loyalty-22554: March 1, 2018

8 Salmon: https://www.adweek.com/digital/new-report-shows-just-how-significant-amazons-reach-in-ecommerce-is/: July 16, 2018

9 Retail Dive: https://www.retaildive.com/news/why-researching-online-shopping-offline-is-the-new-norm/442754/: May 17, 2017

adopt gamification strategies within the next five years[10] (Boston Retail Partners).

Digital and Television
Clickbait statements talk, too, of the "demise" of television, but that medium was also seeing digital as a companion.

By the numbers:

Twenty-eight percent of adults told Nielsen in 2018 that they "sometimes" used a digital device like a phone or tablet while watching TV[11]. But 45 percent said that they used a second screen "very often" or "always."

Only 12 percent reported that they "never" used another device while watching TV.

Digital had further integrated with television with the introduction and adoption of smart TVs. A smart TV is a traditional television set with integrated Internet and interactive "Web 2.0" features that allow users to stream music and videos, browse the internet, and view photos (Wikipedia).

Now on to even more digital innovation and what it means for marketers.

---

10 Boston Retail Partners: https://www.iflexion.com/blog/the-retail-cmos-guide-to-gamified-shopping/: Oct. 30, 2017

11 Techcrunch: https://techcrunch.com/2018/12/12/nielsen-the-second-screen-is-booming-as-45-often-or-always-use-devices-while-watching-tv/: Dec. 2018

Chapter Four

New Technology

New Tech and Interfaces
Onto the scene have come voice interfaces; reality that is augmented, virtual, and mixed; the Internet of Things (IoT); artificial intelligence and machine learning, among others.

Each has been talked up to the extreme. Some matter now. The others? Not so much.

Let's define terms, starting with voice and then going alphabetically, and provide some more information for us to gauge importance.

Voice
A voice-user interface (VUI) makes spoken human interaction with computers possible, using speech recognition to understand spoken commands and questions, and typically text to speech to play a reply (Wikipedia). A voice command device, such as an Amazon Echo, is a device controlled with a voice user interface.

"Voice user interfaces have been added to automobiles, home automation systems, computer operating systems, home appliances like washing machines and microwave ovens, and television remote controls," the site said. "They are the primary way of interacting with virtual assistants on smartphones and smart speakers."

A pioneer in this category described to me why voice is different.

"The great thing about voice and conversational UI (user interface) is that it's the first big consumer tech trend where it's not relying totally on technology," said Dave Isbitski, Chief Evangelist, Alexa & Echo, Amazon. "Think about that for a second. The web, mobile, desktop apps, all of them, and even social media in some respects, have required a new technology curve to be understood. But everyone understands how to have a conversation, voice is very natural, and those who are good communicators, not necessarily technologists, are creating some of the best experiences today.

"This opens up the ability to have these voice-driven experiences created by people who may not have been part of that process in the past. Being able to tell a story and have an engaging conversation that feels human-like are powerful skill sets in this new voice first paradigm."

But should we care now? Let's look at usage rates.

Smart speaker penetration climbed to 20 percent of U.S. Wi-Fi households in 2018[12] (comScore).

---

12 comScore: https://www.comscore.com/Insights/Blog/Smart-Speaker-Penetration-Hits-20-Percent-of-US-Wi-Fi-Households: April 11, 2018

One in 10 Americans planned to buy a smart speaker in 2018[13] (Consumer Technology Association).

When it came to purchasing through smart speakers, only two percent were doing so as of mid-2018[14] (The Information).

Eighty-nine percent said that they'd like to see a product on a screen before a voice assistant orders it. Because of that, we have witnessed the introduction of such devices as Amazon's Echo Show and Google's Home Hub.

"It's no longer just this invisible interface anymore which is great," said Sheryl Kingstone, 451 Research's Vice President, Consumer Experience & Commerce. "All of a sudden we realized that it can't be blind and we have screens on those speakers. Those are the hottest devices. That's a cross-channel experience. You're going to put something in with your voice and it (the search result) is going to show up as an image. And no one was really buying on the smart speakers because you couldn't visually see what you were doing.

"There's a difference between shoppers and buyers. Where voice comes into play is with transactions. Look at groceries. You are reordering things that you do from second nature over and over and over again. You're getting milk. You're getting (printer) ink. You don't necessarily

---

[13] Washington Post: https://www.washingtonpost.com/technology/2018/11/21/i-live-with-alexa-google-assistant-siri-heres-which-you-should-pick/?noredirect=on&utm_term=.1f35e635af43: Nov. 21, 2018

[14] The Information: https://www.theinformation.com/articles/the-reality-behind-voice-shopping-hype: Aug. 6, 2018

have to shop for them. Those are things where you can easily put them on a shopping list or order on Amazon and do it in a voice scenario."

We'll delve much deeper into voice in the chapters to come and learn more from Isbitski and others.

For now, let's move on to other innovation.

Artificial Intelligence

Artificial intelligence (AI) is the ability of a digital computer or computer-controlled robot to perform tasks commonly associated with intelligent beings (Britannica).

Said the encyclopedia: "The term is frequently applied to the project of developing systems endowed with the intellectual processes characteristic of humans, such as the ability to reason, discover meaning, generalize, or learn from past experience."

This sounds futurist, but it is happening now. As an example, in an effort to better stock individual stores with merchandise that local clientele desires, retailer H&M is using AI to analyze returns, receipts and loyalty card data to tailor the merchandise for each store.

Some see this tech as good. Others don't.

Overall, and despite the downsides that they fear, 63 percent of respondents polled by Pew said they were hopeful that most individuals will be mostly better off in 2030, and 37 percent said people would not be better off because of artificial intelligence[15].

---

15 Forbes: https://www.forbes.com/sites/gilpress/2018/12/15/ai-in-2019-according-to-recent-surveys-and-analysts-predictions/#401e88ac14c3: Dec. 15, 2018

AI was projected to boost profitability in retail and wholesale by nearly 60 percent by 2035[16] (Business Insider).

But there are warning signals. Approximately 75 percent of customers reported that, as technology becomes more pervasive, they wanted more human interaction, not less. And yet 64 percent felt companies had lost touch with the human element of their interface with customers[17] (PwC).

Augmented Reality

Augmented reality (AR) is an enhanced version of reality created by the use of technology to overlay digital information on an image of something being viewed through a device (such as a smartphone camera), as defined by Merriam-Webster.

"AR works by employing computerized simulation and techniques such as image and speech recognition, animation, head-mounted and hand-held devices and powered display environments to add a virtual display on top of real images and surroundings," according to Techopedia.

For this category in particular, the promises have far exceeded the use.

"It has been a slow build," Ryan Spoon, ESPN Senior Vice President, Digital and Social, told me. "So now the question is what are the kind of breakout examples of

---

16 Accenture: https://www.accenture.com/fr-fr/_acnmedia/36DC7F7 6EAB444CAB6A7F44017CC3997.pdf: 2018

17 PWC: https://www.strategy-business.com/article/Closing-the-Gap-between-What-Consumers-Want-and-What-They-Get?gko =e2226: April 11, 2018

things working to drive consumption? What can be tied to hardware that we already have?

"I think that's where you get things like Pokemon Go (a mobile game) that become just absolutely enormous very quickly (powered by smartphones)."

Retail appears to be fertile ground for this type of tech.

Sixty-one percent of shoppers preferred to shop at stores that offer augmented reality over ones that don't[18] (Retail Perceptions).

Fifty-five percent of shoppers agreed that AR makes shopping more fun and exciting (Retail Perceptions).

Internet of Things (IoT)

The Internet of things (IoT) is the network of devices, vehicles, and home appliances that contain electronics, software, actuators, and connectivity which allows these things to connect, interact and exchange data (Wikipedia).

"IoT involves extending Internet connectivity beyond standard devices, such as desktops, laptops, smartphones and tablets, to any range of traditionally dumb or non-Internet-enabled physical devices and everyday objects," according to a posting. "Embedded with technology, these devices can communicate and interact over the Internet, and they can be remotely monitored and controlled."

IoT has become mass through wearable devices that are worn on the human body (Techopedia).

---

[18] Retail Perceptions: https://www.businesswire.com/news/home/20161018005039/en/New-Study-Explores-Impact-Augmented-Reality-Retail: Oct. 18, 2016

"This type of device has become a more common part of the tech world as companies have started to evolve more types of devices that are small enough to wear and that include powerful sensor technologies that can collect and deliver information about their surrounding," the site reported. "A wearable device is often used for tracking a user's vital signs or pieces of data related to health and fitness, location or even his/her biofeedback indicating emotions."

Examples are Apple Watch and Fitbit, among others.

Approximately 50 million were expected to use a wearable device at least once a month in 2018[19] (eMarketer).

While that is a big number, it might be a small opportunity for marketers.

"Wearables have a lot of hype in the marketplace today, as it relates to the consumer experience and shopping," said Sheryl Kingstone, 451 Research's Vice President of Consumer Experience & Commerce. "If you really think about it, are you going to transact on your watch? It's not happening."

Will consumers continue to use the wearables they own? That remains to be seen. In a survey, nearly a quarter of respondents who own a wearable or smartwatch no longer used it. About 30 percent of those said that they quit using their wearable because they had reached their goal. Another 20 percent put aside the device because it

---

[19] eMarketer: https://www.emarketer.com/content/wearables-still-far-from-mass-adoption: Dec.17, 2017

was ineffective in helping them achieving their aim[20] (Rock Health).

Machine Learning

Machine learning (ML) refers to the capability of a machine to improve its own performance (Merriam-Webster). It does so by using a statistical model to make decisions and incorporate the result of each new trial into that model. "In essence, the machine is programmed to learn through trial and error.

"The term was conceived in the 1950s — about the same time scientists begin to use artificial intelligence (AI) for the simulation of intelligent behavior in computers. Although contemporaneous, the two technologies are notably different: whereas AI generally refers to the capability of a machine to carry out tasks as a human would, ML specifically denotes a computer application used to process and learn from data, as exhibited in a self-driving car's ability to detect and process nearby objects. Other common applications of machine learning involve Internet search personalization, fraud protection, and identity security — all of which require a machine to learn particular behaviors."

Nearly half (49 percent) of the businesses that took part in O'Reilly's mid-2018 survey indicated they were in the exploration phase of machine learning and had not deployed any machine learning models into production.

---

20 Rock Health: https://rockhealth.com/reports/healthcare-consumers-in-a-digital-transition/: 2018

That compared to 36 percent who said they were an early adopter (models in production from two to five years), while 15 percent considered themselves sophisticated users (models in production for more than five years)[21].

Netflix is in the latter category. By providing better search results in part led by machine learning, the company estimated that it was avoiding canceled subscriptions that would reduce its revenue by $1B annually[22].

Mixed Reality
Mixed reality is the result of blending the physical world with the digital world, as defined by Microsoft.

From the company's website: "Mixed reality is the next evolution in human, computer, and environment interaction and unlocks possibilities that before now were restricted to our imaginations. It is made possible by advancements in computer vision, graphical processing power, display technology, and input systems."

Microsoft said that the term mixed reality was originally brought forward in a 1994 paper by Paul Milgram and Fumio Kishino, "A Taxonomy of Mixed Reality Visual Displays."

"Their paper introduced the concept of the virtuality continuum and focused on how the categorization of

---

21 O'Reilly's: https://www.datanami.com/2018/08/07/its-still-early-days-for-machine-learning-adoption/ : Aug. 7, 2018
22 Forbes: https://www.forbes.com/sites/louiscolumbus/2017/07/09/mckinseys-state-of-machine-learning-and-ai-2017/#5c7a707d75b6: July 9, 2017

taxonomy applied to displays. Since then, the application of mixed reality goes beyond displays but also includes environmental input, spatial sound, and location," Microsoft reported.

We will go into great depth on mixed reality later in the book when we get insights and direction from Microsoft's Lorraine Bardeen.

Over The Top (OTT)
Over the top (OTT) is a term used to refer to content providers that distribute streaming media as a standalone product directly to viewers over the Internet, bypassing telecommunications, multichannel television, and broadcast television platforms that traditionally act as a controller or distributor of such content (Wikipedia). The term is most synonymous with subscription-based video on demand services that offer film and television content.

Over the top services are typically accessed via websites on personal computers, as well as via apps on mobile devices (such as smartphones and tablets), digital media players (including video game consoles), or televisions with integrated smart TV platforms.

Here are the stats:

By 2018, OTT devices were in 59.5 million homes, up 17 percent year-over-year[23] (comScore).

---

23 comScore: https://www.aaaa.org/wp-content/uploads/2017/07/ComScore-State-of-OTT.pdf: June 26, 2018

Netflix, YouTube, Amazon, and Hulu were the "big 4" services and comprised 75 percent of time spent streaming OTT (comScore).

Connected TV viewers were mostly persons under the age of 34[24] (Nielsen).

Homes with streaming devices were also 30 percent more likely to be higher income, earning more than $100,000 per year (Nielsen).

The obvious implication for marketers is that some eyeballs aren't where they used to be, resulting in the need to modify the marketing mix.

Virtual Reality
Virtual reality (VR) is a computer-generated reality that projects the user into a 3D space (*PC Magazine*).

"Using a stereoscopic headset that provides a completely immersive experience, the virtual reality (VR) system is operated by the user's head and hand movements or a physical control unit, the latter commonly used with virtual reality games," the publication said. "In the early days of VR, data gloves tethered by wires to a computer were used to track hand gestures.

"The very first virtual reality systems were created for pilot and astronaut training, employing a physical housing that looks like the inside of a cockpit. Extremely costly

---

[24] Nielsen: https://www.nielsen.com/us/en/insights/news/2018/the-connected-tv-experience—transforming-the-living-room.html: June 26, 2018

and still being used, they provide a totally realistic experience that simulates taking off, flying and landing."

Is it the time to sprint off to do VR? Maybe.

But fewer than a third of consumers thought virtual reality features were important and 61 percent of retailers said it was of no or minimal interest to shoppers (Bazaarvoice).

Actions To Take — or Not Take

Of course, it's key to not only understand the technology, but also to consider whether and how to integrate one or more rather than creating silos.

Warning: mistakes will get noticed.

"Let me lay out one of the biggest challenges — our customer may be starting on a different device than a mobile phone," Ben Reubenstein, POSSIBLE Mobile CEO, told me. "One could start their experience with a voice device in their living room, or they could have come to us first through an app. And then they want to add in a voice experience with an Alexa and Echo or (Apple) HomePod, whatever that may be. So I think there are going to be more complicated user journeys, and that we need to consider what entry vector we have.

"And then how do we determine who that user is so we can provide them with the most personalized experience that we can, and they're getting what they expect? By that I mean if they bought a subscription to a piece of entertainment, you want them to be able to access that piece of entertainment easily on whatever device they choose and minimize friction to authentication (being signed in or otherwise identified)."

Yes, the options to consider have increased. So, too, have ways that we should look at what was here before.

"I think the phone and the app will continue to be a linchpin and actually start to provide more information to the other devices," Reubenstein said.

For sure, these data points were a snapshot in time and directional at best. But one thing is certain — to ignore them is to set yourself up for failure.

Chapter Five

How ESPN Tackles Other Screens and Interfaces

Much More Than TV

ESPN executives surely and wisely pay homage to cable television. It was there four decades ago where the sports network was born and quickly prospered.

However, they won't bet the network's present or future solely on it.

That's because eyeballs have migrated to other screens — and the adoptions of cord cutting, including OTT — had reduced the traditional pay-TV service by 33 million[25] (eMarketer). By one count, ESPN had lost nearly 13 million cable TV subscribers since its 2011 peak.

That only tells part of the ESPN story.

The network reported a TV and digital audience that nears 100 million Americans per month.

ESPN Digital was by far the world's leading sports digital platform, averaging 115 million users a month. ESPN

---

25 eMarketer: https://www.wsj.com/articles/viewers-cut-the-cable-tv-cord-faster-than-expected-1532452053: July 24, 2018

was No. 1 in sports in average minute audience, total minutes of usage and total visits.

The ESPN mobile app continued its position as the No. 1 most popular sports app, and ESPN Fantasy — including football, baseball, basketball, hockey and ESPN's highly popular Streak game (giving fans the chance to predict winners) — was again the top provider of fantasy sports in 2018, with more than 20 million fans.

ESPN+, the company's latest effort around streaming video, reached one million subscribers in fewer than six months despite a $4.99 per month service charge.

Everything and Nothing Has Changed
"Our mission statement is the exact same as it was when the company was founded," Ryan Spoon, ESPN's Senior Vice President of Digital and Social, told me. "And it is to serve sports fans, anytime, anywhere. The definition of anywhere and that expectation from the fans is the thing that has changed.

"So in 1979, it was television. You get to the early 2000s, it is more channels, but still predominantly television with the emergence of the Internet and I would argue it's not mobile now. That's what the Internet is. It's still the Internet. It looks different. It's now on 5 or 6 inch devices. It's immediate and we are no longer serving web pages. We are serving video or streams and so forth."

By 2018, ESPN had made significant programming inroads well beyond television.

Take a look:

SportsCenter on Snap, short episodes produced each morning for consumption on Snapchat (a multimedia messaging app), increased ESPN's reach for fans 18-24 by 33 percent over TV alone (50 percent for males 18-24) with a daily audience of 2.5 million and 17 million per month. In addition, 71 percent of its viewers did not consume any ESPN core offerings.

The audience of ESPN's YouTube channel was 40 million uniques per month with 31 percent engaging this way under 25. In the last six months of 2018, time spent on the video channel viewing was up 78 percent vs. 2017.

On Instagram, a photo and video-sharing social network, the ESPN and *SportsCenter* accounts combined to grow followers 25 percent to a total of 25 million.

ESPN debuted live shows on Twitter with plans to double the offerings in 2019. The biggest draw on the social network was the NFL Draft with three million views.

On Facebook, across the ESPN and *SportsCenter* pages, engagements were up 48 percent year-over-year while on Twitter the increase was 32 percent.

Anytime, Anywhere

"Our motto says anytime, anywhere," Spoon said. "You can't do that unless you reach them where they are and so we are across all screens, all devices. That's a pretty important part of the strategy.

"I have a pretty firm belief that you have to tailor the experience and experience meaning the look and feel, the product, content, aesthetic, all those kind of things, specifically for the platform. And platform is oftentimes a mixture of hardware and software."

I asked Spoon whether viewers are seeking out more ESPN outlets or looking to replace one like cable with another.

"Selfishly I hope there is no sole experience with ESPN," he said. "But before you can have deep multiple relationships with ESPN, we have to reach you somewhere. That is how we begin a relationship.

"I think the way that you grow someone's relationship with the experience, with the brand, with ultimately driving usage and sustained engagement, means some sort of utility or enjoyment."

Chicken Or Egg Around Audiences

Does ESPN follow audiences — or create them?

"There are examples of us doing both and everything in between," Spoon said. "I do think there are times that it makes sense to enter when something is scaled. And if you do that, it's obviously crowded and the way that you hopefully win and earn share is with quality. There are examples where an audience might be scaled but a product might not have. So you would be betting on a product in the larger ecosystem. Apple Watch is a good example where we were in early.

"Then there are things that we believe will be scaled but probably not in the near term. And the balance there is we think things like AR/VR become significant and scaled, and there is general belief that at some point it will. We need to think about the balance and say, 'Okay, whether it is or not today, we need to have an understanding and opinion of strategy and emerging expertise on how does this work, how it would relate to us when those times come right.' But that doesn't necessarily mean that we need to go to market with consumer products. We need to think about experiments and tests."

It's a mistake, Spoon told me, to think that success is determined by how many experiences you create.

"Quality always wins," Spoon said firmly. "And that pertains to any job. Whether you're creating the content, creating a product, you're distributing the content, marketing it, whatever that might be.

"It is far easier to achieve quality when you do fewer things, and you focus on making them as fantastic as they can be. To create great content for Instagram, it's not just taking a picture. It's video, storytelling. There are stories and narratives and so forth. It takes a lot more effort and thought, but I'd rather have fewer of them in ways that are captivating and engaging. I don't know the best way to say it other than just a general mantra, and that's fewer things done better."

Those lacking imagination might say that with its still massive television audiences that ESPN should stay in its lane and look to build from there. Spoon, a former collegiate swimmer at Duke University, isn't one of those. He is constantly looking to make the next big splash.

Chapter Six

Neiman Marcus: A Century-Plus of Retail Innovation

Differentiate or Else
To believe that Dallas-based Neiman Marcus first discovered innovation in its second century is to make an error approximately the size of Texas.

One can go all the way back to the day it opened in 1907 to see evidence of the retailer's forward thinking and acting.

It was the first to offer upscale fashion to the state's wealthy, according to Wikipedia. Despite the Panic of 1907 that appeared weeks later, Neiman Marcus was immediately profitable.

In 1927, Neiman Marcus premiered the first weekly retail fashion show in the United States.

Since 1939, Neiman Marcus has issued an annual Christmas catalog, which often gets free publicity from the national media for a tradition of unusual and extravagant gifts shown but not sold in its stores.

At one point, the Neiman Marcus Christmas catalog carried the distinction of being the item most stolen from recipients' mailboxes, prompting a Chicago postmaster to suggest the company switch to enclosing the catalogs in plain brown wrappers.

Neiman's fantasy gifts in the Christmas Book have included a $20 million submarine, mummy cases that contained an actual mummy, seats from Ebbets Field (the former Brooklyn, N.Y. home of the baseball Dodgers), and a $1.5 million Cobalt Valkyrie-X plane; the most expensive item was a Boeing Business Jet for over $35 million (Wikipedia).

iPhones Get Way Too Much Credit
"A company like Neiman Marcus didn't manage to survive one hundred and 10 plus years without being innovative," Scott Emmons, the longtime head of the company's innovation lab (or 'I Lab'), told me. "It's not like innovation just got invented over the last 10 years because there were iPhones."

Yes, on one hand, you can argue that Neiman Marcus has been there, done that. But these are extraordinary times for the retail industry. Brick and mortar stores by the thousands are shutting down. Businesses are needing to compete based on not just price, but on such factors as the ability to deliver purchases in two days or less and through the use of technology that digitally puts such things as eyeglasses on one's face, a dining room table in one's house, and product reviews in the palm of one's hands.

"What we're seeing is how quickly the new disruptive ideas keep coming at businesses, and their efforts to keep up with that rate of change, be more agile, and be able to bring new ideas to the table faster," Emmons said.

The Origins of the Lab
The lab was born more than 10 years ago out of the need to create structure and process to the concept of company change.

"For me, what I really was tasked with was innovation that involved bringing technology to bear to solve problems, and figuring out how to seamlessly intertwine that with a Neiman Marcus experience, not just bolted on but to actually have it make sense," Emmons said. "Also, to be part of the luxury shopping experience, and to be on brand and all those things.

"The 'I Lab' was not created to be where all innovation was born. I like to think of it as more of a center of excellence where all those different groups that either need innovation or need to participate in the innovation process and not actually deliver it, have a place to go, and we can be the connecting point for that."

Among the innovation brought to market by Emmons and his colleagues:

- The Memory Mirror, a screen and camera combination that enables shoppers to see outfits from 360 degrees, and compare clothing options side-by-side. It also remembers what customers have already tried on, thereby providing a level of personalization that meets today's desires.

- Digitization of the brand's exclusive lookbooks.
- Intelligent mobile phone charging stations that proved to be both secure and an enabler for shoppers to stay in stores longer.

Like Suits and Dresses, Not Everything Fits
"There is a real temptation to go out and try that bright and shiny thing just because it's cool and everybody is talking about it, and there is all kind of buzz around it," Emmons said.

"But in the end, you go back to the simple question of what kind of projects should we be tackling. Does it solve a real problem? Or let it evolve from being a solution looking for a problem to something that can solve a problem that you've identified that you have. That's how I look at it. You can go do those avant-garde shiny projects and you're going to get a lot of attention and you're going to have the press talking about. Maybe that's a good thing, but that's not our goal."

As you can imagine, for years, Emmons has been pitched on a wide variety of what are loosely and many times inaccurately (or at least prematurely) called solutions.

"There are way too many things we could do," he said. "It is sort of a process to funnel those ideas down to a manageable list of things that you could actually go try. I don't have a magic checklist or silver bullet. I feel we still have room for improvement in that process. It's evolving."

Emmons' excellent track record has been considered when management approval was requested for funding or other resources for new initiatives. Invariably, the subject of expected return on investment was broached.

Establishing A Needed Return On Investment
When it comes to ROI, one size does not fit all.

"I think the type of projects that we work on are varied enough that those metrics tend to be different," Emmons told me. "If you're working on an RFID project, maybe our metric is did we get our level of inventory accuracy to 'X' percent and because our inventory accuracy was better, we lifted sales by this much. You can apply actual traditional lift measurement to see how well something is performing.

"Then you have other types of experiences that have never been done before. And the amount of work it takes to actually tie it back into your transactional systems is large. And so it may be worth it just to try that experience and see if the customers like it, and observe how they interact with it, and sort of take a test drive and not necessarily have a defined ROI on it."

Emmons is bullish on voice interfaces and assistants, but he sees the tech as one component that has issues standing on its own.

"It's obvious that voice is going to be one of those ways you're going to interact with the technology and in some cases, it's a great way to do it," he said. "In other cases, maybe not so much. When I'm looking for inspiration and shopping, I feel like that's a very visual thing. Voice is not going to be able to deliver that component to me. But if I need to order Boston K cups (from Boston's Best Coffee) or something like that, it's just fine for that."

Defining A North Star

The North Star remains the ability to treat each Neiman Marcus customer as an individual.

"We are on the journey to where every interaction is a personal interaction," Emmons said. "There is work to be done to get there. We as a company and marketers in general realize that while we can use personas and have interactions based on past history, and all those things are useful and have their place, the closer we can get to a truly personal relationship with that customer, the better.

"Neiman Marcus' VP of Customer Insight and Analytics (Jeff Rosenfeld) calls personalization 'the new loyalty' and that's what we're marching to. That involves collecting data around the customer and that involves making sure that you have the customer's permission to collect that data. It's also making sure that you're doing it without breaking any statute and doing it legally and honestly and openly and protecting that data and being a good steward of the data. You need responsibility to get that personal relationship."

If you wonder whether Emmons has just been in the right place at the right time — no industry has been ripe for innovation more than retail — stop wondering. Long before his Neiman Marcus days began in 2006, he exhibited his chops, successfully designed and implemented time and billing/job costing systems for the finance department of an information services consulting company that had more than 500 employees.

"As to the question of whether there are some people who should not innovate, there are opportunities across the board," he told me.

Chapter Seven

Personalization: Catering To An Audience of One

Where's The Beef?
The day that I as a vegetarian stop receiving meatball sandwich offers from businesses that know me will be the time that I say bravo to personalization efforts.

Until then, I ask, ' Where's the beef?'

Sure, this is a challenge with hard-to-answer questions. Here are just a few:

- How do your customers and prospects define personalization? Is there a consistency or would responses be all across the board?
- When does personal cross a line and become creepy?
- Is personalization ever going to be perfect, and, if not, is relevant good enough?

Nearly nine in 10 of Americans were willing to have various details of their activity tracked by a brand in exchange for a more personalized and relevant relationship with the brand or loyalty program, according to Bond Brand Loyalty's 2018 loyalty report[26].

More than two-thirds of marketers felt that those in their profession, on average, were not getting personalization right. A full 65 percent would grade their own personalization efforts as a "C" or lower.

McKinsey points to a lack of understanding of the very term.

"Personalization is teetering on the edge of the buzzword precipice," it wrote in a 2018 perspective piece. "As companies rush to embrace it, the concept is increasingly invoked as a solution to everything even as what personalization itself means becomes ever more vague."

The top-shelf marketers couldn't care less about an all-up definition. They just want to understand their consumers and address needs and wants.

"We talk about rising customer expectations," said Sheryl Kingstone, 451 Research's Vice President of Consumer Experience & Commerce. "What we've been really talking about are the three C's — convenience, context and control.

"With convenience, they want to see fast, easy, and frictionless. With context, they want it personalized for me. With control, they want to interact and engage on their terms. What the consumer wants actually is all of that combined."

---

26 Bond Brand Loyalty: https://www.bondinsights.com/welcome-to-the-loyalty-report-2018/: 2018

Like Emmons, Expedia's Aaron Price talks about a line not to be crossed.

"Personalization is an overloaded term," the Senior Vice President of Global Marketing told me. "I think that algorithmically-driven or machine-managed sort of curation is a path that allows businesses to present their best information to any customer as the first thing that they see and you can optimize for both parties at same time. We want to be in the business of putting things in front of people that are more likely to be sold. From that perspective, it is highly critical that that happens.

"The Internet's creepy view of personalization is something that I would say we all aspire to avoid. That's trying to get to exceedingly narrow responses to any customer base on highly, highly personal or seemingly personal information. That kind of stuff is not what we would intend to do or want to do."

Reading and Reacting To Signals

In an interview for *The Art of Mobile Persuasion,* Google's Jason Spero implored us to identify and react to what he called signals that consumers send us.

"Where we are with marketers?" he said to me in 2015, repeating my question. "There are different points of the crawl, walk, run continuum. Many marketers are working on the most basic mobile experiences. The first generation of mobile experiences was cut and paste desktop experiences with smaller weight images. No video and no Flash (a multimedia software platform).

"Where we've gotten to is (some) marketers have come to understand that I want a different experience when I'm on this (a mobile device) than when I'm on this (a personal computer). Now you've built a mobile-specific experience if you are any good. You start to ask questions about signals. You start to be able to say, 'How do I want that mobile experience to change if I'm within a mile of a Pizza Hut (and am looking for pizza)?' Marketers are trying to find which of those signals are relevant to them."

Of course, this was on my mind when I reconnected with Spero for this book.

"I think we're doing better with the signals," he told me. "I would say it's a range of things but I'll name a few. I think we understand better what proximity means and what location means. I have any number of different relationships with a user based on time of day and location.

"Just using the simplicity of those signals, we can customize our UX (user experience) to understand if someone who is in our store has a certain need state. Is this someone who is near or someone trying to find that store? Or is it someone who's probably not looking for a physical store experience in this moment?"

You have a great match when a consumer who is willing to give information in exchange for value meets a smart marketer who is equipped with sophisticated tools and has the wherewithal and guts to personalize.

"I think we have signals based on depth relationships with brands because so many of us now store personalization," Spero said. "I don't order Thai food from the best

Thai restaurant in my neighborhood. I order Thai food from the restaurant that stores my preferences, remembers what I like, and makes it easy with one click ordering."

The Google executive offered up one more scenario to illustrate the importance of reading signals.

"Let's look at a hotel-oriented company trying to book rooms," he said. "It's important to know if I'm in New York City at that moment looking for hotels in New York versus if I'm someone who is in Los Angeles looking for hotel rooms in New York.

"One of them says I probably need a hotel room in the immediate future if not tonight. The other says that I'm planning a trip to New York and I want to see a broader set of options so please show me your full catalog. Whereas if I'm in New York looking for hotel rooms in New York, you should show me a narrow set of options, presumably around me and presumably with availability tonight. We've gotten much better inferring that from a lot of the signals that a consumer will give out."

Much better is good. Mastery, i.e. no meatball sandwich offers, would be better.

"I've seen research on all the touchpoints that a consumer takes on the way to a journey like trying to research where to get a burrito in a town that you don't know," Spero told me. "You see consumers engaging over devices, sometimes through an app, sometimes through the web. Our job as marketers is to try to stitch all of that together.

"Add to that the complexity that sometimes we're typing, sometimes we're talking to our device, sometimes we are inside a social media environment. Other times we are using traditional ways of getting information. And the consumer expects us to understand her and serve her needs holistically and to be faithful. They expect you to remember what part of her journey that she's already taken and not show her the pieces that she's already nailed down, but to build on that."

In other words, the same-old marketing, including mass messaging blasts, just won't work.

"This is a fairly fundamental shift for anybody who wants to offer value to her as she's doing her research," Spero said. "Whether that's YouTube where she could see beautiful images of hotels and destination or someone to help her get the best price. They all need to understand her better and understand where she's been on that journey to date. And be honest, I don't think we have yet delivered as an industry the right tools for marketers to stitch all of that together."

Chasing The Wrong Motivation?

It's not specifically meatball sandwich messaging ineptness that riles global marketer Thom Kennon. He is critical of overall personalization efforts by marketers, telling me that we've been chasing the wrong motivation.

"In the last five, six, seven years, I think we talked about personalization and to get someone's attention," he said to me. "I think we're kidding ourselves. Everything we do in human life is driven by need. I don't think there's a (customer) journey. I don't think there's a (marketing) funnel (the long-held belief that consumers go in a path from awareness to purchase). People are in their own little rivers with one thousand shores. And those thousand shores include all sorts of things that pop up that satisfy their need for their day, throughout their week, in their world, in their life.

"Our job as brand strategists is to know enough about what those very specific needs are. We're talking about not using data to target people with advertising. It's that insight about their specific needs. We need to get better at mining and then articulating a specific insight that's human at a specific moment in time that we can say to ourselves, 'Okay, great, what do we do with that insight? What can we do in a brief and create some sort of content or app or website or service or information or something that we can constantly engineer into the moment of consideration at that needs stage?'"

This leads to extreme adjustments that Kennon is convinced we need to make.

"It's the fundamental formula for the science of new marketing," he said. "It's a radical departure from the typical way and typical tools with which we understood how to get (brand or product) consideration. It's not about personalization, per se.

"When people see personalization, two things happen. They either say, 'They're trying to prove they know me because they've got something on me' or cynically freak out because 'You're using my data against me'. I think it's about accessing this need and giving people their own control and access to their own choices about all these decisions about need fulfillment."

Preferences, Permission and Privacy
In the 1940s, psychologist Abraham Maslow's identified a hierarchy of human needs, spanning the areas of physical (such as the need for water), security (including the need to be safe), social (such as the need to be loved), ego (including the need to be recognized), and self-actualization (such as the need for development and creativity).

Maslow wrote of commonalities that, if considered, are useful for marketers. Still, there is no escaping the fact that individuality comes into play when we attempt to persuade — or even reach — people to consider our services or buy our products.

Even the well-intentioned seasoned professionals often struggle with delivering the right message at the right time on the right platform.

Kennon foresees a near future where marketing is tied to permission.

"We get to this idea of invited interruption," Kennon said. "People will not commission a set of beer brands that I only want to hear about, or a set of cosmetics brands that I only want to hear about, or a set of technology brands. People will set up their preference centers, and people will be monetizing their own data. I really do believe that is happening in the next three, four or five years. The whole proposition is based on this new battleground. How do we earn our way into this kind of invited interruption?"

Kennon argues that if we stay on the current course, attempts at personalization will fall short.

"People will tell you that they like being able to see things that are relevant to me," Kennon said, "but everybody knows the feeling of your search for a pair of summer deck shoes in May and for the rest of the summer on Instagram, all you see is advertising for these crummy little Dexters that reminds you about the ones you bought seven weeks ago."

In Kennon's mind, a preference center reduces the misfires and provides a level of satisfaction missing from today's efforts.

Google's Jason Spero said the work to date has only brought us part of the way there.

"I think we've gotten much more aware of the value exchange with the consumer to use cookies and different types of things to try to understand people and serve their needs better," Spero told me. "I think we understand that the consumer has to opt in to all of that. Anything we do to improve the experience has to be with explicit consumer permission. That's the foundation of what we're building.

"What you can start to see if your consumer sees value from you, the consumer can give you permission to engage with them across the web and apps, across the search experience and YouTube experience and the (Google) Maps experience. You can start to connect the dots. You can start to put together all of these engagements to be able to personalize those experiences once you have permission. Where I think it gets tricky is when the consumer is not giving that explicit permission. We have to be responsible as an industry."

Some espouse a future where each individual owns his or her data and barters it in a value exchange. Those hyping this suggest that it will happen quickly.

I, for one, won't take that bet.

The Verdict Is Mixed
McKinsey's final word on personalization is mixed.

"The truth is that personalization at scale is both easier and more complex than most people expect," it wrote. "For example: getting value from personalization can be fast and only requires the thoughtful usage of what the business already has in place. But scaling personalization requires the integration of advanced technology, people, and processes, a complex choreography that depends on strong leadership and clear vision."

Chapter Eight

Expedia: Traveling Into the Future

Let Mobile Be Your Guide

When I was growing up, a travel agent was a person who researched, recommended, and booked trips.

Today, the agent is more than likely a mobile device.

Google said that 48 percent of U.S. smartphone users were comfortable researching, booking and planning a trip on a mobile device. That number jumped to over 70 percent who always used their smartphones while traveling to research activities or attractions, locate shopping areas and restaurants, or look up directions.

Companies like HotelTonight have built strong businesses around the new dynamic, one where the consumer is in charge and often making last-moment decisions that have impacted price, capacity, and property market share.

Mobile's Importance To Industry Leader Expedia

Expedia, the world's largest travel brand with more than $11 billion in annual revenue as of Q3 of 2018[27], sees

---

27 Expedia: https://ir.expediagroup.com/static-files/81e17b27-aa5c-4a59-b7de-4aaf158a8aa0: Oct. 25, 2018

more than half of its customers engaging via mobile. And it's not just for discovery or trip research. More than one in three bookings are made this way, according to the company.

"Today, its ubiquitous," Aaron Price, Expedia Senior Vice President of Global Marketing, told me. "Almost everyone on the planet has a mobile device so it's become really front and center for our interactions with customers."

Per Expedia research, 68 percent of Generation Z used a smartphone in the so-called inspiration phase when they were determining where to go. Another 61 percent of Millennials did so.

Approximately two-thirds of younger travelers were undecided on a destination when they chose to take a trip, illustrating an opportunity for brands to influence through relevant content and advertising.

Forty-six percent of Gen Z used a smartphone in the research phase, 1 percent higher than the usage by Millennials, according to Expedia.

When it comes to booking, otherwise known as marketing's all-important last mile, 32 percent of Gen Z employed a mobile device, 1 percentage point less than the usage of Millennials.

However, It's Not All Mobile

The importance of mobile cannot be overstated. It is front and center, but in the U.S., at least, it is neither everything nor for everybody.

"The challenge is that people are now interacting with companies oftentimes through more than one device,"

Price said. "In many cases, it's up to three or four devices (such as smart assistants and wearables).

"Getting information about customers and how to best handle them can be a bit harder to piece together. That problem is very much out there for many companies and certainly for us."

With the new interfaces and consumer preferences come even more challenges.

Price and Expedia colleagues must choose when and how to evaluate a new technology. And when an effort is underway, additional decisions need to be made as to when to double or triple down and when to exit an under-performing trial.

"It is primarily what we call test and learn," Price said. "Trial and error would be the right way to categorize it. We put a lot of tests out there to see what it is that people want or like about interacting with us.

"We tried a number of different avenues in the last year like Amazon Alexa skills. We also actually have been making some investments in chat interfaces, mostly in Asia where chat is more popular and pre-voice, if you will. We have a text-based version similar to voice chat, where people can ask relatively open-ended questions and we have technology on the back end to answer the questions and be available for them."

Addressing Needs Through Technology
I asked Price whether the mission for Expedia is to be innovative or to serve the customer.

"It's both," was his response. "Our mission is to revolutionize travel through the power of technology. We want to serve customers ultimately who wish to plan and travel. It's what do the customers need and what do the customers want as technology evolves?"

Price views the consumer journey this way:

"People in this world are more and more defining either shopping patterns, purchasing patterns, or information gathering patterns that work well for them, but there's no one single right way," he said. "And maybe the best analogy I can give you is a long time ago there were only three or four TV stations, and everybody watched what was on that was preprogrammed for them. Now, anyone can watch any content they want to. The audience's demand for that kind of content has not diminished. It has significantly expanded at this point.

"But the sheer number of people who are doing any one thing at any one time has diminished greatly. There are no 100 or 200 million (viewer television) programs but there are lots of one or two million view pieces of content."

Of course, those at the travel company must guard against falling for so-called shiny objects, those "solutions" that are far from proven but have buzz or a feature that could put them in the consideration set.

"Everyone has to be relatively sober-minded when evaluating the possibility of what might come in the future and realize that for all of us who are trying to predict what can happen in the future, we're all partially right and partially wrong," Price said. "At least that's in my experience.

"I feel almost there's an inevitability that voice search will become an important way for people to just find information anywhere, whether it's in travel or anything, and it may not be fully there today. But that doesn't mean that we should wait until it becomes fully evolved before we actually try and figure that out. There are probably bigger, more speculative questions around what will happen with things like virtual reality, augmented reality, and some more nascent technologies."

How Expedia Assesses Results

A Fortune 500 company such as Expedia surely views its activities with an eye on return on investment. However, not everything needs to have an immediate monetary benefit.

"At the end of the day, what I look for is some element of nonlinear response," Price said. "Whether its VR, whether it's voice, whether it's anything else, before you truly are worried about monetizing something, what you're really trying to figure out is whether or not there's a response from people to whatever it is that interaction mode, or that technology or that feature.

"I would call it a huge success if we get lots of people, thousands or tens of thousands of people doing voice search or some of our (early) VR experiences. And if you got that response pretty quickly or over time, that response starts to grow. In a kind of nonlinear way, it tells me that there's a customer need, a people need for these kinds of things that really allows us to invest further and it ultimately would benefit the company as a business. The first question is do you get signals from your customers that this is something that they want to use."

As an example, Expedia is in the midst of a multi-year process to determine how to bring value through virtual reality. Through in-house Expedia Labs, it has built multiple VR experiences more for understanding the technology rather than making a mass splash.

"The initial thought is we can take people to exotic destinations and have them experience them in a virtual way." Price said. "It's early days for us to understand whether that is something that is kind of interesting for people or whether or not that would truly inspire them to want to take vacations. I'm of the opinion that a virtual experience is kind of the first step and then the real experience is the one that people truly aspire to."

Let's Find A Deal
Expedia Labs runs hackathons and co-creates new experiences with partners. One such effort was Skymuse that in 2016 enabled consumers to find the best prices from around the web. Every flight search performed by users of Expedia, Orbitz, Travelocity, and CheapTickets was analyzed in real time by Skymuse to determine if it was truly a deal.

Using an outlier detection algorithm, Skymuse compared each search result flight against historical flight price data to determine if it is a real deal. These prices were then displayed on Skymuse for a short period of time, with links to the search on the website where they were found. Flight prices changed quickly, so there was an element of urgency.

Skymuse provided learnings for Expedia, but like many tests, it didn't lead to a broad release.

Never Lift A Finger

Serving consumer and business travelers only partially describes Expedia's job.

In such a competitive industry, where price often trumps all else, the company succeeds in part by bringing innovation to its travel partners.

One interesting endeavor was Expedia's partnership with Palace Resorts, a luxury all-inclusive resort brand in Mexico and the Caribbean. The property presents itself as one that offers guests a world of luxury and amenities, worry-free, without lifting a finger.

To sell the concept, a digital marketing campaign was launched in 2018 that utilized eye-tracking functionality to create personalized recommendations to a consumer without them ever having to lift a finger.

"Never Lift a Finger" was brought to life with a desktop and mobile-friendly microsite featuring a video quiz that matched site visitors to their ideal Palace Resorts property and location using the eye-tracking technology.

Visitors to the microsite were presented with two parallel videos around a variety of themes, including trip type, activities, experiences, cuisine and entertainment, and were asked to use their eyes to make selections. Upon entering the microsite, users were prompted to grant access to their web camera, which enabled them to opt in for the eye-tracking software experience. Users who did not wish to use the eye-tracking software could manually select their preferred videos throughout the quiz.

As the videos played, software tracked interest and preferences based on which video the user paid attention to the most, or the direction of their gaze. An on-screen beacon served as an additional guide for users, showing them where they were looking on the screen.

The campaign ran across Expedia, Hotels.com, Hotwire and Travelocity in the U.S., Canada, Mexico, Latin America and the U.K., and users were driven to the microsite from display advertising, homepage takeovers and e-mail.

Live Long and Prosper
Eye-tracking. Virtual reality. Voice assistants. What's next?

Price does rely on his imagination and, at least to some part, lessons from years ago.

"I think back when I would watch Star Trek when I was much younger, and many of the things in Star Trek seemed like pure science fiction," he told me. "Many of those things have become reality. For example, they used to walk around with pads that were insanely thin but could control the entire spaceship. Those things became reality in mobile phones and tablet computers today, and are almost ubiquitous."

"I expect the customer journey to get even more complex as voice search becomes a bigger part of it," he said.

Price would suggest buckling up for that trip.

Chapter Nine

Twitter: Creating Emotional Connections

Building A Relationship

Brands have long been keen on creating relationships with customers and prospects. As you've surely picked up by now, it's the how, the what, and the where that have seen the most change.

Stacy Minero has been one of the most important change-makers.

Minero's experience in content marketing and what she calls emotional connection pre-dates Twitter's launch in 2006.

From a seat at top agency Mindshare, she worked with networks and brands to develop compelling programming. Among the assignments was teaming with Fox to create a 25th episode of "24", and with Bravo to create an after-show tied to 'Project Runway'."

"It was so far back that you had to email in your question," she remembered. "There was no social. I saw that the world was moving from traditional advertising that people had to endure to content that people wanted to watch."

Be Here and Everywhere?
Now as Head of Content Creation at Twitter, Minero advises brands to understand every platform, but not necessarily be everywhere.

"When it comes to brand marketing, obviously our partners are creating these holistic communication plans," she told me. "I used to do that. I think that every platform and channel has a role and a superpower and Twitter's is to launch something new. If you want to reach the most influential audience that is receptive, you go to Twitter. It's where the conversations start and where those messages can spread. And where what happened on the platform can influence what happens off platform.

"I think it's less about whether you're on Twitter and what you do on Twitter. Not every brand should do a purpose-driven campaign that is trying to mobilize consumers and create a mission. Not every brand should necessarily have a voice where they're trying to be clever and funny and interactive. Every brand should find their most valuable audience and use the platform in the right way, in a targeted way, but not do all things for all customers."

Maximizing Opportunities With Twitter
For many brands, Twitter is a vehicle to tap into a worldwide user base of more than 300 million and to use the platform's access to influencers and causes.

More than 90 percent accessed Twitter on mobile screens, according to the company, but screen dimensions aren't the most critical factor.

"It's more about the behavior than the screen size," Minero told me. "We think about the fact that people are more likely to either scroll or swipe than they are to stop by a piece of content. We think about things like engineering the front end of a piece of content to create stopping power.

"(That's unlike) in traditional TV, where you have what we call the opportunity to romance the reveal with a narrative arc that culminates with some payoff."

Minero counsels clients to optimize for sound-off viewing, ensuring that people can process the brand's message perhaps with captions for dialogue or visual key messages or key product benefits that are going to resonate with a consumer and drive recall.

Time certainly is of the essence, demanding storytelling and visuals that quickly grab the viewer.

"Emotion is the currency for brand advertising," she said. "Think about how you can create that emotional connection very quickly."

Friends Again

Bank of America's *"Friends Again"* campaign succeeded following this path. To create awareness and consideration for its peer-to-peer app, the brand tapped into social creators rather than brand content to tell the story primarily to a younger audience.

"They created a whole holiday called 'Payback Friend Day,' and took the stigma out of owing people money," Minero explained. "You go out to dinner, and with check-splitting, somebody is a winner and somebody is a loser. Or you might see this with fantasy football.

"The brand tapped into the insight about friendships that that might fall apart due to money issues and converted that insight into this culturally-relevant campaign. They used the social creators that had connections with their fan bases to not only gain attention but also to drive conversation."

Activating The Audience
Campaigns in all mediums often have a goal of turning the passive into active.

Nike and adidas have been especially imaginative on Twitter, engaging members and turning on-the-ground events into happenings viewed globally.

"When we think about emotional currency, one of the big ways to do that is to design participation," Minero explained. "It's moving people from viewing to doing and then giving them something that is rewarding and valuable. You can do that through content, you can do that through experiences."

First, in 2017, Nike created "Breaking2", an attempt for elite athletes to break the two-hour barrier for running a marathon. The number of people tuning in to the live stream on Twitter was nearly eight times higher than the broadcast audience of the New York, Boston and Chicago marathons. In total, 13.1 million watched the attempt live via Twitter, making it the company's largest brand-powered, live-streaming event.

"It was cool because you saw all the tweets from the people who are watching on Twitter, " Minero said. "And then you have this curated timeline where you had all these journalists and sports broadcasters weighing in minute by minute, weighing in on what was happening on screen.

"'Breaking2' created a sense of urgency. I would say also anticipation because there's an outcome — either the marathon record will be broken or not. You are driving tune in around this anticipation. They also used Twitter Tools. You can 'heart' to get a reminder when the race is going live or when key moments were happening."

The following year, adidas developed "Friday Night Stripes", the first live streaming series of high school football games on Twitter. The sports brand chose teams with star players and "fused sports and culture," Jeff McGillis, Vice President of U.S. Sports for adidas, said in a press release.

Minero said adidas scored because it combined video, passion, and exclusivity.

"They saw the white space in video content, they saw the conversation around football at this passion point," Minero said. "They created this live streaming experience where you could consume something that you couldn't consume anywhere else."

Dunk In The Dark
One of the most memorable brand efforts on Twitter was during Super Bowl XLVII in 2013 when Oreo and its digital

agency reacted to a blackout during the game with the tweet, "Power out. No problem. You can still dunk in the dark." The message was retweeted 10,000 times in one hour, according to *AdAge*.

Since, anticipation has grown for the next breakthrough moment.

Minero cautions brands about forcing it.

"I think about real time in the context of right time," she told me. "I think if you empower your content creators or your community managers to take advantage of moments that are relevant for the brand, it's a smart thing to do. I think chasing viral moments is not a smart strategy. Thinking about your brand position or strategic territories is the right thing to do."

Interestingly, some brands have built upon the concept of user-generated content (UGC) to entice customers to take part in user-generated product (UGP).

"If you think about Mayochup, which is a combination of mayonnaise and ketchup, Heinz put a Twitter poll out there and said if you get to 500,000 (participants), we're going to put these products on shelves in your local stores," Minero said. "And that created a whole gamification of that campaign. And they got a billion (media) impressions within 48 hours."

Oreo also stood out in 2017 by offering customers $500,000 and an opportunity through #MYOREOCREATION to devise new product combinations.

"People would tweet about them and post about them on other platforms," Minero explained. "And on Twitter, they would send back to certain consumers a playful gif (image) that showcased the combination and the suggestion that the consumer had. It felt like a reward and that the brand was hearing them. They felt celebrated and also gave them currency to share with their friends and followers.

"This was a great way to use a campaign to not only get attention but to create brand advocates. The finalists were kettle corn, pina colada and cherry cola. It was the unexpected combinations that kept people interested in what the outcome would be."

Humans and Machines

As to where we are headed, Minero views machines as helpful but not the end-all.

"You're never going to take humans out of the creative process," she said. "That's because ideas come from understanding mindset and motivation and universal human truths. But I think technology will continue to up our game in terms of optimization, everything from understanding what hair color resonates in a video to the type of like product and packaging you should showcase in a shot.

"There's going to be a lot more innovation and disruptors. I'm not sure how it will play out. I do think that great stories that are rooted in human insight and strike a cultural chord will be sustainable forever."

Chapter Ten

Amazon: Giving Your Brand A Voice

Returning To Yesteryear
In an era replete with taps and scrolling, Amazon's Dave Isbitski considers the introduction and evolution of voice technology a positive return to yesteryear.

"It's interesting to live through the desktop revolution, web, mobile, seeing social come on, and, and now voice, " the Chief Evangelist, Alexa & Echo, told me. "I do feel that it's that next disruption. And, to me, it is back to human-to-human interaction.

"Every one of those ways, I felt like the technology enabled us to communicate a little bit better. We could reach more people with mobile. We could reach people where they are. And with social, we didn't have to be wearing a business suit. With voice, it's about business the way it used to be when you would just walk into a store, and you knew the people there. I think technology has robbed us of that."

Voice may be growing in popularity — by 2018, one-in-six Americans owned a voice activated smart-speaker, per Edison Research and NPR[28] — but that doesn't mean that businesses know what to say and how to say it.

"If your company has grown up as a startup in the mobile space, you may have never had a voice," Isbitski said. "Some of these companies don't even have a place you can dial in. It's a live chat, or a customer support center, or something like that."

Other brands flail when contemplating meeting customers and prospects on voice-enabled devices. Some who've had a voice in traditional advertising are unsure whether that effort effectively transfers to this newer technology.

It's Simple – Simplify

Isbitski urges marketers to simplify matters.

"Really where you should start thinking is if I had my customer in a room right next to me and I wanted to have a conversation," he said. "Because voice is so natural and simple to do, you find the types of questions and engagements that you get with your customers are really much more meaningful."

Amazon is a leader in the space, but hardly the only innovator. Assistants from Google, Apple, and others are popping up on nearly anything and everything, as proven at CES 2019 when even a voice-enabled toilet was shown.

---

28 NPR: https://www.npr.org/about-npr/577007267/jan-2018-smart-audio-report: Jan. 10, 2018

Jeff Hasen

Google has developed five insights on voice technology as shared in a blog post in 2018[29].

1. Voice is about action.
"When people talk to their Google Assistant, they're usually trying to get something done," wrote Scott Huffman, VP, Engineering, Google Assistant. "Assistant queries are 40 times more likely to be action-oriented than Search, with people asking for things like 'send a text message,' "turn off the lights,' or 'turn on airplane mode.'"

2. People expect conversations.
"When people start using voice assistants, we often see very simple commands," Huffman said. "But very quickly, expectations go up in terms of complex dialogue. We might see 'Weather Chicago' typed in Search, whereas with the Assistant we see much longer and more conversational queries like 'What's the weather today in Chicago at 3 p.m.' On average, Assistant queries are 200 times more conversational than Search."

3. Screens change everything.
"The world hasn't completely shifted to voice, nor do we expect it to," Huffman wrote. "Screens bring a completely new canvas for conversational AI, where we can bring together voice and touch in an intelligent way. So when you ask for a pasta dough recipe, you can get visuals of

---

29 Google: https://www.blog.google/perspectives/scott-huffman/five-insights-voice-technology/: Aug. 21, 2018

what the dough should look like while the Assistant reads you the steps along the way."

4. Daily routines matter.
"You can access the Assistant almost anywhere you are throughout the day — on the phone, in the car, or on a speaker in the living room," Huffman explained. "So it makes sense that when people use the Assistant, it's largely driven by their environment and what they're trying to accomplish in their daily routines."

5. Voice is universal.
"One of the most exciting things to witness about digital assistants is that even though the Assistant is a new technology, it's incredibly easy to adopt," he said. "There's no user manual needed, and people of all ages, across all types of devices, and in many different geographies can use the Assistant. Because of this, we're finding that Google Assistant users defy the early adopter stereotype — there's a huge uptick in seniors and families, and women are the fastest growing user segment for the Assistant."

It Can't Be About Voice Only
As is the case with each technology discussed in this book, voice's success is dependent on it not being viewed in a silo.

"'Voice first' doesn't mean 'voice only,'" Amazon's Isbitski told me. "Voice will always be, in the short term, the fastest and most natural way for people to communicate with your brand or product. But it doesn't mean they'll be throwing away your website and your mobile app. In fact, it can add to those experiences tremendously.

"For example, let's say I'm using your website to purchase a new financial service offering. My mobile app may tell me the current mortgage rates or information about the product, but it's far easier to just ask and have a conversation around the service or if there are any other services that you might recommend."

In the relative early days, queries often are random with information sought on such facts as the age of a celebrity, the year a song was released, or how to prepare Brussels sprouts.

"Ad-hoc queries have tremendous value in a voice driven experience, for example just asking for something like, 'Show me all of the checks I've written in the past six months over $500' gives incredible utility," Isbitski pointed out. "The same is true for commerce. While I may create an initial order through your website or mobile experience, in the future, if I want to reorder something, just being able to ask to 'reorder cat food' or 'get my favorite dinner again' will offer tremendous value and speed offer traditional interfaces.

"But, none of the underlying technology that you've already created for mobile and web are changing in these scenarios. You are simply creating a new conversational experience, an HTML-like layer that sits on top of the interface between your customer and your brand allowing voice to become a new transaction end point for you. It's additive, not subtracting."

Voice and Sales
What's not to like? For one thing, there certainly is a ways to go before voice interaction meaningful drives product sales.

An early 2018 report by The Information said that only 2 percent of owners of Alexa-ready devices used them to make a purchase in 2018. And of those who did use Alexa to shop, 90 percent did not try it more than once.

Later in the year, in a recap of end-of-year holiday activity, Amazon said that customers' use of Alexa for shopping more than tripled in 2018 versus the previous year. But no additional visibility was offered.

Usability testing by Nielsen Norman Group conducted in 2018[30] found that "both voice-only and screen-based intelligent assistants work well only for very limited, simple queries that have fairly simple, short answers. Users have difficulty with anything else.

"For most interactions, people will easily figure out that they are not speaking with a human. Although users project human-like qualities onto them, they have relatively low expectations for these assistants and reserve them for black-and-white, factual questions," the company said. "Even though the main hurdle is probably better

---

30 Nielsen Norman Group: https://www.nngroup.com/articles/intelligent-assistant-usability/ :July 22, 2018

natural language and dialogue processing (an inherently hard problem), many smaller scale issues could be fixed with more thoughtful design."

Like Google and Apple, Amazon has developed comprehensive tutorials and best practices for marketers to accelerate their efforts.

Act and Participate

Isbitski implores marketers to do what they've always done — act upon consumer insights.

"Ask how familiar somebody is with the technology," he said. "Are they new or been using a device since 2014 and have six or seven Echos in their home? That impacts expectations. "

Even those most active will utilize voice some but not all of the time.

"People aren't going to throw away their phones," Isbitski said. "We should look at this as another way to converse with them. I know I'll still do my taxes with a web browser. There are certain things I'll do on mobile and then there's certain things I just want to ask Alexa to do like reorder triple A batteries."

To those early into digital transformation, voice interfaces fit into a sensible mix.

"We always said from the early days that voice is king," said mobile pioneer Laura Marriott, the first global president of the Mobile Marketing Association. "Voice is the way that people interact with their device. It's going to continue to explode. I love that you can get through voice exactly what you're looking for or the information that you need instead of having to scroll through lists and lists of data.

"Voice appeals to every demographic whether you are five years old or 95 years old. Everyone knows how to use it."

Isbitski, whose career stops have also included positions at Microsoft and Johnson & Johnson, closed with one more solid piece of advice for marketers needing to understand the technology shift.

"I've always been someone who likes to 'live in the future' and I've been fortunate enough to have roles where I'm working with cutting edge technology and then going out and speaking to others about what the impacts are," he said. "That means constantly looking at new technology trends, learning how they apply to our lives, and in the end teaching people what that future may look like. It helps generate people's ideas and then they run with it.

"For a marketer, tech adoption is no different than any other topic. Keep on top of the latest buzz and trends, look at what the community is saying, whether through social media or at networking events, and start to use the latest technology in your own life. Not being a late adopter can have tremendous benefit here. I've talked to marketers who have been using Alexa since 2015 and the ideas they have for what conversations are possible are very different than someone who has never used a device at all. Using early versions of technology today can give you a vision for what tomorrow may look like."

Chapter Eleven

Microsoft: The Recipe To Get Mixed Results

Looking Back To Look Ahead
To assess the present and future of reality, Microsoft's Lorraine Bardeen recommends that we first take a history lesson.

"Any transformative technology encounters challenges to mainstream adoption in its early lifetime, such as cost, size, comfort, and technical barriers," Bardeen, General Manager Studio Manager, Mixed Reality, told me. "We've seen this all before with the very first computers, the Internet, and mobile phones.

"Just like the evolution of other similar technology, we expect momentum for the technology to begin in the commercial space and then trickle outward to consumers."

The progression has led Microsoft to introduce the HoloLens Development Edition that is the first fully self-contained, holographic computer, enabling users wearing an untethered headset to interact with high-definition holograms in their world.

Illustrating where we are in the adoption curve, applications are mostly deployed in the business world, although there have been some instances where consumers have been exposed to the technology and benefits.

"While we've made incredible advances possible across consumer and commercial productivity, education, and entertainment thanks to capabilities provided by computers, we are still constrained by the need to primarily interact with computers via screen-based input," Bardeen said. "It's interesting to think about how humans are actually experts at interacting with 3D environments and objects in the physical world in which we live, but we haven't been able to extend this capability when interactions are entirely behind screens – until now, with mixed reality."

More Human, Not Less
Greg Sullivan, Director of Communications at Microsoft, told me that digital interfaces are being developed to be more human, not less.

"We see this as evolving the interaction model between digital and humans," Sullivan said. "We're moving from cryptic commands with a computer that were one dimensional to a two-dimensional graphical user interface. That's more like it is in the real world. We are in a march to make the interaction model more human."

Bardeen offered up use cases to show the value of mixed reality.

"Using holograms, you can pin your digital content, such as apps, information, and even multi-dimensional videos, in the physical space around you and the workspace in front of you, so you can interact with them in the same ways that you interact with other physical objects," she said. "Mixed-reality experiences will help businesses and their employees complete crucial tasks faster, safer, more efficiently, and create new ways to connect customers and partners."

This all should interest marketers, but it's the business sector that primarily can gain from the tech today.

Microsoft said that FirstLine Workers are more than two billion strong, the first to engage customers, represent a company's brand, and see products and services in action.

"You can imagine how customers across industries can leverage the potential of this technology," Bardeen said. "For instance, it enables Firstline Workers to feel more effective as they are able to understand data in context and simplify their workflows to extend their own ability. For businesses, this means that they are reimagining their business processes by leveraging modern, unified, intelligent and adaptable solutions that bring together vast amounts of data across the organization.

"In fact, recently we shared how Toyota is using this technology to improve their paint thickness quality testing, reducing what was a day-long process for a team to one that takes four hours and one person."

Museum Visitors Meet A Pioneer Through HoloLens

HoloLens has been in the hands — or, more accurately, *on* the heads — of museum visitors in New York. Microsoft partnered with the Intrepid Sea, Air & Space Museum to unveil an installation on Defying Gravity: Women in Space, a mixed reality experience at the Intrepid that shares the stories of previously unsung women who've made critical contributions to the United States space program.

Located beneath the Space Shuttle Enterprise, the experience uses Microsoft HoloLens headsets to take visitors on a journey through the history of women who have played important roles.

Astronaut, physician, and scientist Mae Jemison, who was the first woman of color in the program, shares these stories, as well as her own. The tour is led by her hologram, created for the installation by Microsoft's Mixed Reality Capture Studio.

More than 100 cameras captured Dr. Jemison simultaneously from varying angles so visitors can see and hear a life-sized version of Dr. Jemison in mixed reality.

"It's important to note that we are not using new technologies just for technologies' sake, but in order to enhance the ways in which we tell stories to reach our current and ultimately new audiences," Marc Lowitz, Intrepid Museum Senior Vice President, Business Development, told me. "These technologies prompt the senses and not only do visitors learn, but they 'feel'.

"One of our primary goals at Intrepid is to engage audiences through different storytelling strategies. We host traditional exhibitions with texts and objects, have hands-on zones for touch-based experiences, computer-based interactives, and more. As we especially want to appeal to and grow our youth and millennial audiences, it's critical to add new technologies that are relatable to that audience. We are always seeking to improve the visitor experience and vary the ways that we story tell."

Lowitz's answer to a question about ROI?

"The number of visitors who actually get to participate at any one time is relatively small, (but) in the aggregate we expect thousands to partake," he said. "These type of experiences also create buzz from media and consumers that is proportionally greater than the number who actually participate, and create a positive halo overall for the museum. By way of example, on Smithsonian Day, when we introduced Defying Gravity, we had one of our highest attendance days in the museum's history.

"Beyond buzz and press attention, these type of projects are also critical for institutions like the Intrepid Museum in attracting new funders."

Mixed Reality Won't Shove Other Realities Out of the Picture

While certainly bullish on mixed reality, Microsoft's Bardeen forecasts a place for all flavors of reality, including augmented and virtual.

"We believe that these are not separate concepts, but rather labels for different points on a mixed reality continuum," she said. "The reality is that if one succeeds, then the ecosystem succeeds, and we're interested in further education and adoption of the spectrum as a whole.

"Specific to marketing, this technology allows marketers to engage with their audiences in new interactive and immersive ways. The possibilities truly are limitless."

Chapter Twelve

How To View Innovation

Don't Expect Perfection
Scott Emmons, longtime head of the innovation lab at Neiman Marcus, drove change at Neiman Marcus until he left in 2019. It was neither mindless nor random nor perfect.

"There are multiple definitions of innovation," he told me before his departure. "The obvious answer is what are new ways to look at your business problems and apply new ways of thinking to solve the problems for your customers. That's in the end what it is, and it may be incremental or maybe it's disruptive and there are huge changes. And then there is everything in between.

"I put simple rules to it. Is it going to solve a real problem for the customer? Is there something we can do with the way a customer interacts with us that we can create less friction and there's new technology that can help go solve that problem? That's number one for me and, number two, because we have always been a high touch, relationship-based kind of retailer, and that's sort of the mantra, will the technology help deepen that relationship, or is it going to get in the way of it? If I can get those two things answered positively — that it is going to solve problems and does it help our relationship with the customer — then we can go off and start looking at is it supportable? Is it cost effective? Is there an ROI to it?"

"There Are Opportunities Across The Board"
I asked Emmons whether marketers should be innovative or professionals who implement the change identified by others.

"I feel like it's my job and my responsibility to listen from wherever they (innovative possibilities) are coming from, and try to help that person to connect with the right resources in the company to determine whether it's something we should be doing, or something we should put in the parking lot for now," he said. "I go around the world and meet lots of new solution providers that are doing things in retail and brings back a list of things that are possible. That's one place the ideas come from.

"But I get tons of input from all sorts of leadership across the company who are going out and doing similar things, and talking to people and meeting people and looking at understanding the problems they're having in their area of business. And these ideas may go into the hopper. And you've got on-the-line sales associates who are face-to-face with customers every day. They certainly are providing input to that hopper as well. And then there's this never-ending barrage of communication from solution providers that claim to have the next big thing."

Measuring Success

In my research, I failed to identify anyone or any entity that has a definitive checklist or scorecard that provides a thumbs-up or thumbs-down on an innovation effort.

Sure, there is science to it — think about number of users and time spent, for instance — but there are also learnings and strengthened teamwork that are more difficult to quantify.

"I think there's a success measurement of a team being able to successfully deliver something to market for a new technology that is undervalued," POSSIBLE Mobile's Ben Reubenstein told me. "A brand working with their agency or tech partner and doing something in a reasonable amount of time and getting something to market that is well received is actually a huge demonstration that the team, whether they pick the right technology or not, will be successful in the future.

"Let's say you jumped in real early and you did something with augmented reality and Unity (a cross-platform game engine). Guess what? When ARKit (Apple's software-development kit for creating AR apps) rolled out from Apple, you could have been there with a little step ahead. Maybe you didn't pick the right tech the first time out of the gate in terms of where that experience might live, but the next time you will be ready for it."

Beyond Monetary Benefits

Reubenstein has run disruptive businesses for more than a decade, including Colorado-based Double Encore, a mobile app development company working with big brands that was sold to WPP's POSSIBLE in 2014.

Prior, he was one of the earliest enthusiasts around the iPhone, producing a mobile web application in 2007. It was a basic Internet Speed test called iNetwork Test. When native applications were announced, the app was pushed to the app store and reached No. 22 on the U.S. charts. By the end of 2018, there were close to two million apps available in that one store alone.

Reubenstein has always put the proper emphasis on revenue generation, but he has additional metrics in mind when evaluating a project.

"When you do something early, you can get some earned media, some social mentions, some good articles, more than just your own press release," he said. "I think there's value in getting out there. You're also going to have a really engaged audience that is hungry for this new tech. You'll know what they thought about it and whether they found it useful.

"I do think you need to bring users in who probably wouldn't have found their way to the tech because it's too early and ask them what they thought of it and whether they would adopt it down the road."

Listen To Your Customer and The Challenges

While the newness of products at such conferences as SXSW and CES is often noteworthy, frequently we are left asking ourselves whether the invention addresses a problem or not.

Reubenstein has noticed that, too.

"I think for really innovative stuff to come out, you need to listen to your customer and the challenges that they are having," he said.

"Look at Tide Pods. When they were introduced, they were the most expensive way to buy detergent and they were engineered for the elite customer. But they became popular in the laundromat because it was a convenient way to carry the detergent around. That was a total surprise to the folks who designed it."

The Need To Think Broadly
One title that Aaron Price has not had in a 17-year career at Expedia is pro with many hats. But he certainly could make a case for the moniker, having served as application engineer, release manager, director of technology, senior director of technology, Vice President of Technology, Vice President marketing regional brands and integration, and now Senior Vice President of Global Marketing.

His advancement shows that he has many answers, but he will be the first to tell you that he hardly has them all.

He has discovered that it's a mistake to look at all technologies the same way.

"I think there are probably bigger, more speculative questions around what will happen with things like virtual reality, augmented reality and some more nascent technologies," Price said.

It's The Consumer Who Will Decide

Whiteboard sessions conducted by technologists, marketers and strategists are necessary and often valuable. However, the ultimate yay or nay on a product or service comes much later.

"We are following the basic marketing tenants and technology is going to continue to evolve," said Laura Marriott, a leader in introducing mobile marketing and other tech to the world. "What's interesting is ultimately consumers are deciding what works for them and what doesn't.

"Interactive content, AI around personalization, chatbots, voice search, podcasts, they are deciding that this is what they want because it gets them reputable content, not ads. This is the evolution we're seeing. I don't think that technology matters as much as how the content is being delivered."

Those marketing tenants, Marriott said, are the same that you learned in school or in business.

"You always want to do what's cool and hot and shiny," remarked Marriott. "But it comes back to what is the goal of your campaign. Is it brand awareness or whatever your marketing goals are for your campaign? What is the message you are trying to convey? Then work on what channel or approach that works best.

"It's interesting. I hear a lot this year that AR and VR are going to be the big thing, which is funny because we've been talking about that for a long time. Even though there are some interesting use cases, I still have a tough time understanding how that is a broad market opportunity. It's an example of something that we struggle to fit in a marketing strategy and it's still not there."

"'Lessons Learned' Is A Great Approach"

Of course, while many of the technologies discussed in this book are "new", none employed at this point would make you a first mover. That's not a bad thing.

"We can always learn from the experiences of others," Marriott said. "'Lessons learned' is a great approach. In mobile, we established best practices as a way to expedite the launch whether it was mobile video or mobile advertising or something else. We found the best practices really helped everyone get to the same level playing field and ensured that a brand understood all the elements in the mobile toolkit.

"I think that those are extremely important, particularly when growing a new industry. I'm not sure that it led to much disruption in the early days because mobile itself was so disruptive or using the mobile channel was so disruptive. Consumers want authenticity from the brands that they interact with. And how does best practices play here? Think from your heart and think from your head. It is more basic tenants of being a good human being."

Play The Long Game

POSSIBLE Mobile's Reubenstein cautions against thinking of these initiatives as one-and-done.

"I think the key is to realize that this is a long game and you need to really create engaging experiences and leverage this technology," he told me. "You can't just spend a month here and a month there. You have to be building constantly because software is never done."

And neither is the introduction of new hardware. Count on that.

Chapter Thirteen

The New Breed of Marketer

Getting On The Train

For the last decade or more, I've asked prospective employees in interviews whether they were looking for the type of job that has the regularity of working on a train that arrives in a station every 12 minutes and stays for two more before departing.

The line of questioning has been meant to weed out those who need to do the same thing day after day from those who understand and even embrace change.

Certainly over those 10 years, our professions and professional lives have done the opposite of standing still.

Given that changes now come faster and more often, that train that I refer to can appear headed directly at us. Or at least on some days it feels that way.

"Marketers are doing what they've always done," Google's Jason Spero explained to me. "Marketers want to drive a dialogue with a consumer about the value of the brand. They want to drive awareness of the brand and consideration of the brand. They want to drive intent and purpose to purchase and they want to drive loyalty.

Core marketing is fundamentally trying to do the same thing.

"The tools that marketers need to master and use have gotten more complicated. We are seeing fundamental shifts in organizations based on what used to be called an information technology organization to work more closely with the marketing organization. We've seen a rise in people who have titles like Chief Digital Officer. I think the creative organization which used to just write a brief needs to understand the tools of the trade as well as probably needs to understand how personalization works, so that they could build many different types of creative to serve the different environments and shards of identity that the marketer is going to be able to reach."

I've never found Spero to be someone who aggressively sells his company's products and services. With that in mind, it struck me as smart when he expounded on the virtues of looking inside and outside an organization to get today's marketing done.

"The first thing is to understand is whether this is something you're going to do in house and if so how do you build an organization for marketing in 2019," he said. "The second thing is to look at partners. In many cases, companies like Google and others are offering certain key tools that make it so that the marketer can be a marketer, and so that the data storage and the data analysis and maybe the segmentation can be done via tools that we provide to make that marketer's job easier.

'The explosion in complexity has made the marketer's job harder. But as an industry, we're starting to get our hands around, our arms around, some of the tools that marketers need and provide that to them."

As you would expect, there is a gap between those who have run with today's marketing challenges and those who have run from them.

Gartner research shows that despite the enthusiasm for innovation, marketing's innovation capabilities for it are not up to par. In fact, Gartner's 2018 Marketing Maturity Assessment[31] revealed that while marketing leaders scored themselves an average of 2.3 out of 5 for marketing maturity in innovation, many wished to achieve at least a 4.3 maturity rating.

Only one in every six marketing dollars was being spent on innovation-related initiatives.

Gartner's 2018 Marketing Technology Survey reported that marketing leaders used, on average, 61 percent of their martech stack's capabilities. This emphasizes the need for an adaptable marketing technology roadmap, to clearly define use cases and remain cognizant to the challenges of integrating solutions, people, processes, data and culture in the marketing organization.

"At the individual marketer level, some are doing a better job," Google's Spero told me. "Some have really built holistic models in terms of the value of the engagement

---

[31] Gartner https://www.gartner.com/doc/3880126/gartner-marketing-maturity-assessment- :June 27, 2018

and the role of the different touchpoints. And some frankly are still struggling to get the user experience right or the understanding or pre-populating fields or what you are asking from the consumer on a device."

Global marketer Tamara McCleary argued against the idea that one person must be an expert in all things. The mission, she said, is for marketing to operate as an asset.

"Marketing needs to step up and be a part of business growth versus being a liability," she told me. "There won't be any more lines between marketing and sales. No more siloes. No longer will the role of marketing be relegated to the ugly stepchild chair that happens to be in the meeting at the executive table but not seen as part of the leadership team. That will all change with intelligent marketing.

"There's a pivotal shift, an inflection point. A marketer has to step up and use the technology available to do smart marketing. It's not arts and crafts class anymore. We now have to look at how we are handling our analytics and then what kinds of real insights are we gathering? How quickly are we getting insight to execute on? It's no longer about your hunch."

McCleary said that the modern marketer can neither be timid nor intimidated.

"We are harnessing machine learning and we are acquiring artificial intelligence to help personalize our target market, but we're still in the beta stages," she said. "It's rather clunky and slow and cumbersome. We really need to understand what it is that you want to derive from that data. I think technology is going to drive the business model to morph and change. Human beings are critically important to this."

The winners, she said, will operate with a sense of urgency.

"We don't have 10 years to figure it out, we've got 10 minutes, " she said. "We are all wondering where to place our next step. We are all walking on top of quicksand, and we have to be hyper-vigilant about the steps we take. But at the same time, we also can't hold back because we could be completely disrupted if we aren't moving forward.

"We ask, 'Are we relevant, can we rise to the challenge? Are we able to keep up? How do we innovate? How do we embrace technology and not make the wrong decision?' It is never going to be about the individual again. We will shift from the individual to the ecosystem."

Subject Matter Experts and Silos
During the early days of mobile marketing — think 2007-2010 — one of the most important recommendations that we made to brands was not to banish mobile to a separate island. The channel needed a seat at the table, from planning throughout the process.

The same recommendation comes today when experts in voice, machine learning, data science, et al, must all row in the same direction despite often times sitting on different floors — if not in different buildings.

There's no definitive playbook for this, either, only advice from those charged with making it all work cohesively.

"You don't want to be organizationally siloed, but there are times your experience from device to device or platform to platform actually needs to be somewhat siloed because what makes a great Siri or Alexa app in the future is fundamentally different than a show that is delivered on Snapchat," ESPN's Ryan Spoon told me.

"My hope is that with people's capabilities and interest, they're able to traverse those different platforms because I think … that's more fun from a career perspective. People like agility."

Succeeding At Transformation

You would be out cold if you played a drinking game at most any conference in the last few years and said you would take a shot each time that you heard the term digital transformation.

According to Wikipedia, "Digital Transformation (DX) is not necessarily about digital technology, but about the fact that technology, which is digital, allows people to solve their traditional problems. And they prefer this digital solution to the old solution.

"The transformation stage means that digital usages inherently enable new types of innovation and creativity in a particular domain, rather than simply enhance and support traditional methods."

In her role as Vice President, Customer Experience & Commerce, 451 Research's Sheryl Kingstone closely monitors the adoption of digital technologies and techniques.

"Over the last couple of years, it has changed actually pretty dramatically at the low end," Kingstone told me. "We used to have a large percentage of companies having no plans whatsoever. That has slowly come down and they've moved into the researching and planning phases. So they might not have formally engaged investment dollars being allocated to it. They still researching and planning and they probably have more dollars allocated than they even realize.

"Anytime you have a software investment or process investment, which is what we've been doing for decades, you're in a digital transformation world. The reality is they just don't see it as a formal strategy. It's still very much departmental grassroots."

A common mistake, Kingstone said, is believing that the transformation has a beginning and an end.

"Some companies still feel like they are going to be able to embrace it within one to two years," she said. "The reality is that is the companies that have more formal strategies totally understood that isn't like a diet. You still can't go on a diet for a week and expect something to change your life. You have to change your lifestyle. And it's the same thing with digital transformation. It's an ongoing, consistent investment that you have to change. It's just the goal posts keep moving out."

How so?

"We do not know what the next engagement channel is going to be," Kingstone told me. "That is constantly always changing. It's a never-ending problem."

Or it's an opportunity if your takeaway from that oncoming train is that the light will guide your way.

Just expect an uncharted path and imperfection along the way.

"There is no innovation and creativity without failure. Period," said Brene Brown, research professor at the University of Houston and TED speaker.

Chapter Fourteen

Mobile's Role Moving Forward

Here To Stay

One reason that I wanted to write *The Art of Digital Persuasion* was to ask the experts whether some technologies and behaviors need to be pushed aside to make room for voice interfaces, wearables, and the other innovations that have been introduced.

And, if the answer is yes, which ones go?

Every now and then, I'll see or hear someone forecast the end of mobile phones. Headlines like one in *Information Age* that include the words *the mobile phone is dying* cause me to believe that someone is dumb, trying to be provocative, is looking for clicks and tweets, or to be included in a book. Or all of the above.

Scott Emmons heard the same suggestion in an interview. He remembers the moment well.

"I was flabbergasted because it never occurred to me that anybody thought it was temporary," the former Neiman Marcus executive told me. "You're going to carry your information pipeline and your compute power around with you all the time. And I can't imagine that going away.

"I don't think that I should win any awards for predicting that it it's here for good. It's just going to get better and more ubiquitous, and the interfaces that we use to communicate with our mobile technology are going to get more intuitive and more interesting and more interlaced into our everyday interactions with everything."

Emmons sees that in his Texas house where he has lived since the early 1990s.

"When I moved in, I had a dial-up modem and a computer that could talk to the Internet," he said. "There are probably 50 or 60 devices today around the house connected to the Internet full time communicating, everything from my (clothes) dryer to my swimming pool to my thermostat to my blah, blah, blah.

"All the things are connected. I can access them remotely (through his mobile device), program them, have them adapt themselves to what's going on around me. They've just gotten to be more and more a part of everyday life."

"Everyone Thought We Were Crazy"

Thom Kennon and I go back to 2007, a time when the iPhone was just being introduced and Kennon was watching rapid adoption of all types of phones and exploring the uses of mobile in marketing via his role as Vice President of Digital Strategy at Wunderman.

"We were the ones who were saying — and everybody thought we were crazy when we said it —... let's start thinking mobile first, because of its penetration, because of its promise, because of its personalization. Because of everything," he recently told me.

"The fact was is in emerging markets and in mature markets that that every single day, more and more people were addressable or reachable through the digital web, through laptops, or tablets, now through mobile smartphones. You get a little kid watching movies on his phone. You've got 75-year-old people doing their shopping on their phones. You've got everybody in between doing all sorts of things on the phone with an increasing frequency every day."

That all sounds great, but how effective have we been in marketing through mobile? Kennon gives us a grade of 65.

How have we failed?

"The fact that we're still trying to reach people is funny," he said. "It's like the generals always fight the last war. And we're still trying to reach people. We are still trying to persuade people and to get in front of people using more traditional advertising techniques, processes, strategies, and methods.

"And in the end, the one thing we learned from the last seven or eight years of digital marketing, and increasingly it's true for mobile smartphone experiences, humans hate advertising. So now you have ad blockers. We have huge portions of clicks from big fat thumbs trying to close boxes. We are whistling past the graveyard. We're continuing to try the same old techniques and methods and strategies with diminishing returns."

Caution Flags
Laura Marriott, the first global president of the Mobile Marketing Association, raises caution flags as well.

"We used to say that mobile is different because it is not interruption-based like traditional advertising, for example," she said. "Now I think that we've made mobile messy. We focus so much on advertising.

"I think what we're doing wrong is anytime you bring up a website on your phone, you've got pre-roll video, you've got interstitials and you've got banners. It's just so difficult to get to the content that you're trying to get to. We're trying as vendors, and maybe this is unfair, we're trying to capitalize on as many revenue opportunities as we can and it impacts the brand experience for their target consumer."

That impact, Marriott told me, is hurtful.

"Because if I'm getting the video and that pop up and whatever else, it's actually giving me a negative perception of the brand to follow," she said.

What's the better way to go?

"You look at other brands who are doing campaigns, they start with honesty, integrity and truth," she said. "And you see the authentic brand. They're being more experiential, delivering reputable content and not buying up every possible ad space that they can."

The Role of Apps

I have one word to say about that prediction of the death of mobile apps.

Hogwash.

If you don't believe me, look at the numbers.

There were 194 billion apps downloaded worldwide in 2018, according to App Annie[32].

App store consumer spend in 2019 will surpass $120 billion — double the size of the global box office market and bigger than the global live and recorded music industry, the same source predicted.

That doesn't, however, mean that the role of apps isn't changing.

"I see apps becoming a more a core part of businesses as they realize the power of this device in our pocket," POSSIBLE Mobile's Ben Reubenstein told me. "Obviously, entire companies are based around these apps, unicorn level-sized companies (like Uber), but smaller companies can benefit, too, from creating a relationship with their customers that can more from more than a webpage.

"Apps serve as post-acquisition CRM (customer relationship management). They are a great way to maintain a conversation with your user and create wonderful experiences for them to get a task accomplished."

Some of those accomplishments will come with little to no effort.

---

[32] App Annie: https://www.appannie.com/en/about/press/releases/app-annie-releases-annual-state-of-mobile-2019-report/: Jan. 16, 2019

"The other core thing that we will start to see is more passive interaction with apps," Reubenstein said. "You might install an app (on your phone), but largely interact with it via your voice. With the ability to hook into Siri (Apple's voice assistant), your ability to create experiences that the user can leverage is going to be really interesting.

"For example, for a phone company, or your mobile provider, you will be able to ask the device, 'How much data do I have left this month?' if you are not on an unlimited plan. Or ask, 'When is my bill due?' and get responses back that are our proxy via the app. I think it's going to become more and more common. The interfaces might change, but the solid engineering and Apple are more important than ever."

Cash Will Be Gone By Tuesday
I would be happy to argue the point that the most hyped technology since the first smartphone was introduced is in the area of payments. To believe some, cash was supposed to be gone by a Tuesday in 2012. It wasn't.

It's a fact that Americans are becoming less reliant on physical currency. Roughly three-in-ten U.S. adults (29 percent) said they made no purchases using cash during a typical week, up from 24 percent in 2015, according to Pew[33].

---

33 Pew: http://www.pewresearch.org/fact-tank/2018/12/12/more-americans-are-making-no-weekly-purchases-with-cash/: Dec. 12, 2018

Impressive? That's up for debate. What isn't is this — 53 percent of Americans said they tried to make sure they always have cash on hand just in case they need it.

The largest players – mobile operators, credit card companies, Fortune 500 retailers — have spent years attempting to meaningfully change behavior in the area of digital currency.

Walmart Pay. Apple Pay. Android Pay. Samsung Pay. Dozens if not hundreds of offerings.

The most notable flameout was CurrentC, an app developed beginning in 2011 by a consortium of retailers that came together to form MCX, or Merchant Customer Exchange. Participating retailers included Walmart, Target, Best Buy, CVS, Shell, Olive Garden, Lowes, Michaels, Sears and others.

Of course, 100 percent adoption of mobile payments was — and is — never going to happen. However, there has been relatively snail-paced movement due to a number of factors including fragmentation, lack of consumer awareness, and the so-called solutions not adequately addressing a problem.

Still, the efforts go on.

"I think there's huge room to grow with mobile payments," Reubenstein told me. "Apple Pay, Google Pay, all those things are out there, but we're not seeing them adopted at a high rate. I think there's going to be a lot of disruption in point of sale. And if you're not thinking about making the transaction the most seamless and quickest part of an interaction with a brand, you're thinking about it totally wrong.

"If you're using a legacy point of sale, and you're not accepting new forms of payment, and you're not thinking about the next forms of payment, whether that be Google Pay, Apple Pay, watching what's happening with Venmo, and personal person-to-person or Square cash, you're missing a huge opportunity to improve the customer experience."

Are Mobile's Best Days In the Past?
Early in 2019, there was near panic on the street — Wall Street, that is — when Apple lowered its first quarter guidance by $5 billion driven by weaker than expected iPhone sales. There was debate over whether the cause was a diminishing economy in China, high price points, lack of appreciable improvements in the latest devices that told consumers to sit on the sidelines, smartphone saturation, or all or some of the above.

Regardless, Apple stock dropped 9 percent on the day following the announcement.

Wrote Kara Swisher in the *New York Times*[34]:

"The last big innovation explosion — the proliferation of the smartphone — is clearly ending. There is no question that Apple was the center of that, with its app-centric, photo-forward and feature-laden phone that gave

---
34 New York Times: https://www.nytimes.com/2019/01/03/opinion/apple-revenue-china-innovation.html : Jan. 3, 2019

everyone the first platform for what was to create so many products and so much wealth...

"Now all of tech is seeking the next major platform and area of growth. Will it be virtual and augmented reality, or perhaps self-driving cars? Artificial intelligence, robotics, cryptocurrency or digital health? We are stumbling in the dark."

Purchases will likely pick up when 5G, supposedly bringing connectivity speed 5X of what smartphones have lived on, is finally introduced and benefits are communicated and understood.

"We are at the entrance, we are at the door, we are about to step into 5G," Liya Sharif, Head of Global Brand, Content & Creative Services, Qualcomm, said at Wunderman Thompson's Future Ready breakfast at CES 2019. "5G will be as transformational as the Internet was."

Sharif said beyond speed, 5G will limit latency, and "connectivity will be like electricity.

"The use cases are endless," she said. "5G will open new audiences for us. Movies will be downloaded in one minute. There will be more complexity in the marketing stack and it will require a new level of creativity."

Marriott, the first global president of the Mobile Marketing Association, said that the future is bright.

"I think we've watched the ecosystem change considerably which in itself has brought opportunities and challenges," she told me. "I think the progress has been positive. And there are so many opportunities for brands to connect with their target customers, not just through mobile, but I think mobile has provided us tools that's made marketing better."

Is There Such A Thing As Too Much?

The all-you-can-eat buffet has been described in *Food and Wine* magazine as "the epitome of American gluttony." That title is now in jeopardy.

To hear Apple and Google these days, mobile has become for some like the Bloomin' Onion, or the equivalent of 3,080 calories in one sitting. We know that we are full at 2,000, but we can't seem to help ourselves.

Social networks. Push notifications. Time spent watching videos. Netflix. YouTube. And more.

According to the NPD Group, in 2018 the average U.S. smartphone user consumed a total of 31.4 GB of data each month (Wi-Fi and cellular combined). Cellular data usage among consumers with unlimited plans was 67 percent higher than those with limited plans, per NPD[35].

Ramifications For Marketers

How did we get here and what does this all mean for marketers?

First off, is the present any different than what we could've — or should've — imagined? We have given users unlimited data, high-definition large screens, content to entertain, inspire and teach, and access to almost anything wherever and whenever. Should we have believed

---
35 NPD: https://www.fiercewireless.com/wireless/alarming-unlimited-data-usage-31-4-gb-per-month-and-rising: Jan. 3, 2018

that mobile users who have unlimited plans would be able to stop after just a few bites of mobile's Bloomin' Onion? Did we expect consumers to spend hundreds of dollars on a device to just keep it in their pockets? Have we not conditioned our customers and prospects to come to us on mobile any time and at all times?

Now Google and Apple, whose operating systems were in the hands of 99 percent of mobile users in the U.S., have introduced efforts to enable us to help ourselves. In 2018, Google unveiled tools to help create balance. It said that 70 percent of users wanted help. Just before that, Apple introduced Screen Time, which, via iOS 12, gave Apple customers app and device usage information and lets them limit access if they want to cut down. Screen Time features include activity reports, app limits and new "do not disturb" and notifications controls designed to help customers "reduce interruptions and manage screen time for themselves and their families."

Notable for marketers, iOS 12 gave customers more options for controlling how notifications are delivered. Users are now able to manage notifications to be turned off completely or delivered directly to a special notification hub. Siri can also make suggestions for notifications settings, such as to quietly deliver them or turn alerts off.

Screen Time creates detailed daily and weekly reports that show the total time a person spends in each app they use, their usage across categories of apps, how many notifications they receive and how often they pick up their iPhone or iPad. People can take control of how much time they spend in a particular app, website or category of apps. The app limits feature lets people set a specific amount of time to be in an app, and a notification will display when a time limit is about to expire.

What Are We To Do?
This changes everything for marketers. Or does it? It's always been about delivering value: quality not quantity. The fact that so much time is spent on mobile devices may indicate to some that marketers are succeeding. But the savvy marketer understands that these "limiting" tools give consumers the power to shut off the unwanted features and to curate exactly the individual experience that they want.

This means that campaigns are affected. In a nine-month period ending in March of 2018, just before these limiting "solutions" were introduced, brands sent 300 percent more push notifications than in the previous nine months, according to Adobe. With consumers now having the ability to dispatch pushes away from the home screen, more care and thought is necessary to ensure that those messages sent to consumers are viewed in a timely and actionable fashion.

Program measurement has also needed to be adjusted. Time spent has been a key metric since the iPhone's debut. Clearly, marketers and developers must rethink the idea that it's all about how long they can keep mobile users engaged.

So is mobile going to relinquish the gluttony descriptor back to the buffet? Time will tell. Surely, all-you-can-eat mobile usage works for tens of millions of subscribers. Many are entertained, more productive and enjoy access to friends and family that can't be replicated elsewhere. Plus, their waistlines aren't affected.

It's all about choice and perceived value. The former is definitely be driven by the latter. Now more than ever.

Chapter Fifteen

Even More Innovation

No Space To Fit Everything
If 2.7 million net square feet of exhibit space at the 2019 Consumer Electronics Show (CES) could not contain all of the tech — and it couldn't — it's impossible to cover every innovation in the limited space in this book.

We went this far without mentioning the cloud, robots, and drones, but that time is over.

Before we close, I do want to help with definitions of several more areas worth at least a watch.

Blockchain
Blockchain is a digital database containing information (such as records of financial transactions) that can be simultaneously used and shared within a large decentralized, publicly accessible network (Merriam-Webster).

"The technology at the heart of bitcoin and other virtual currencies, blockchain is an open, distributed ledger that can record transactions between two parties efficiently and in a verifiable and permanent way."

At the time of this writing, I had yet to meet a brand marketer proceeding swiftly down this road.

Chatbots

A chatbot is a computer program or an artificial intelligence which conducts a conversation via auditory or textual methods (Wikipedia).

"Many chatbots rely on machine learning or artificial intelligence (AI) in order to simulate how humans communicate," said Drift, a company with a conversational marketing platform. "More specifically, intelligent chatbots often rely on machine learning, which is when a computer program can automatically improve with experience, as well as natural language processing (NLP), which is when machine learning is applied to the problem of simulating human-produced text and language."

Drones

A drone is an unmanned aircraft that can fly autonomously, as defined by *Scientific American*.

Real estate professionals have been known to use drones to capture shots of a property from multiple angles.

DMNews pointed to four potential marketing applications — drone delivery, drone as advertisements, drones as creative marketing tools, and data collection.

The Cloud

The cloud is a term used to describe a global network of servers, each with a unique function (Microsoft).

The cloud is not a physical entity, but instead is a vast network of remote servers around the globe that are hooked together and meant to operate as a single ecosystem. These servers are designed to either store and manage data, run applications, or deliver content or a service such as streaming videos, web mail, office productivity software, or social media.

Instead of accessing files and data from a local or personal computer, you are accessing them online from any Internet-capable device — the information will be available anywhere you go and anytime you need it.

Robot
A robot is a machine — especially one programmable by a computer — capable of carrying out a complex series of actions automatically (Wikipedia).

Robots can be guided by an external control device or the control may be embedded within. Robots may be constructed to take on human form but most robots are machines designed to perform a task with no regard to how they look.

One area to watch is how robots are complementing or replacing traditional customer service.

Rich Communication Services (RCS)
RCS is a communication protocol between mobile-telephone carriers and between phone and carrier, aiming to replace SMS messages with a text-message system that is richer, provides phonebook polling (for service discovery), and transmits in-call multimedia (Wikipedia).

At the time of this writing, Google supported RCS but Apple did not.

In-vehicle technology
A connected car is equipped with Internet access, and usually also with a wireless local area network (Wikipedia). This allows the car to share internet access and data with other devices both inside as well as outside the vehicle.

By 2019, voice assistants were common in vehicles with more usage an easy bet.

The marketing ramifications are to be determined and early tests were underway.

For instance, at CES 2019, Honda was one entity looking to give brands a way beyond radio, mobile ads and marketing messages to reach consumers in cars. It announced its beta Dream Drive program that introduces a dashboard that rewards opted-in drivers and passengers for using the car's connected capabilities. Drivers can earn points for using the dashboard to navigate to their next destination, pay for gas, order food or make other purchases. Passengers can also get points for listening to the radio or playing games through a Honda app.

Whether significant numbers of people will consent to have their data shared with brands through their connected car is yet to be determined. Honda promises brands "last mile" data showing how their marketing led to sales.

Another area to keep an eye on is autonomous vehicles. A self-driving car, also known as a robot car, autonomous car, or driverless car, is a vehicle that is capable of sensing its environment and moving with little or no human input (Wikipedia).

In summation, if you believe that you need a robot or 24 more hours in a day to process all this information, you are not alone. Given the pace of advancement, both of those scenarios appear possible.

Conclusion

Predicting and Creating The Future
Futurist Michio Kaku forecasts life-changing, even life-saving uses of emerging technology.

"As transportation is digitized in the next decade, driverless cars, guided by GPS and radar, will share our highways," he told Futurism[36]. 'Traffic accidents' and 'traffic jams' will become archaic terms. Thousands of lives will be saved every year."

Let's hope that the prediction is true.

With all due respect to futurists, everyone has an opinion of what's ahead. I wish that we kept a scorecard for all the prognostications offered up at conferences, on the web, on Twitter, LinkedIn, and elsewhere. Certainly a good number of predictions come close. Others, like the one that foresees the death of mobile, are preposterous when delivered.

I recall *Scenes From The Future,* a 2013 McKinsey and Co. painting of an individual's life in 2020[37]:

---

36 Futurism: https://futurism.com/michio-kaku-prominent-futurist-predictions: March 26, 2018
37 McKinsey: https://www.mckinsey.com/business-functions/marketing-and-sales/our-insights/the-coming-era-of-on-demand-marketing: 2013

It reads:

Curious about her friend's headset, Diane taps it with her phone. Both have near-field communications (NFC) capabilities.

Diane's phone prompts her to photograph her face and then displays how the headset would look on her in various colors.

She's then invited to send her photo to her Facebook friends, who are asked to vote among a choice of colors that best suit Diane.

Meanwhile, she received a text alert from Spotify offering a free month's subscription to its premium music service if she buys the headset (the manufacturer's data show she isn't a subscriber).

Friends like the headset in fuchsia, and Diane completes the purchase.

When the headset is delivered the next day, a message asks if she would like to post a "wow" picture on Facebook of her wearing it, with a link for others to buy it as well.

When she meets those friends in person, her cellphone reminds her of the NFC chip in her headset and offers her an additional free month of Spotify's service for each friend who taps and buys a headset.

Every week, she gets a "club gig of the week" message, offering discount access to a venue if she wears the headset when she walks in the door. A club video board welcomes her by name.

When Diane listens to music, Spotify reminds her that the headset manufacturer has brought her this listening experience.

At a gym a few weeks later, Diane gets an opportunity to buy and download an exercise program the gym offers. She can access the program by tapping her phone on a nearby display.

Much of the future that is Diane's experience is here today. McKinsey more often than not nailed it. But it isn't everyone's future.

Real Reality

Here's how futurist Ray Kurzweil sees life in 2023:

"We'll be on the digital web, all the time in virtual/augmented reality," he told *Fortune*[38]. "We won't be looking at devices such as tablets and phones. Rather, computer displays will be fully integrated with real reality. Three-dimensional pop ups in your visual field of view will give background information about the people you see, even a tip that someone just smiled at you while you weren't looking. The virtual display can fully replace your real field of view putting you into a totally convincing fully immersive virtual environment. In these virtual environments, you can be a different person with a different body for each occasion. Your interactions with the realistic virtual projections of other people will also be completely convincing.

---

38 Fortune: http://www.kurzweilai.net/ray-kurzweil-by-2030-full-immersion-vr : Oct. 9, 2000

"Search engines won't wait for you to ask for information. They will know you like a friend and will be aware of your concerns and interests at a detailed level. So it will pop up periodically and offer something like 'You've expressed concern about Vitamin B12 getting into your cells, here's new research from four seconds ago that provides a new approach to doing that.' You'll be able to talk things over with your computer, clarifying your needs and requests just like you're talking with a human assistant. Artificially intelligent entities will be operating at human levels — meaning they will have the same ability to get the joke, to be funny, to be sexy, to be romantic."

Sexy computers. Finally.

There Are No Absolutes
If there's one thing that I've learned in nearly 20 years of working in emerging technology is that there are no absolutes. One-hundred percent adoption is unrealistic. More importantly, it's not the yardstick that we as marketers should use.

The question is whether your customers and prospects are engaged or will be engaged in one or more innovation. If you deem the number meaningful, proceed. If it's low or not even moving the needle at all, move more deliberately. Or move on.

It's impractical, and frankly unwise, to throw your efforts around every new technology mentioned in this book. But standing still is even a worse path.

"Innovation is not an option," Kirsten Ward, General Manager, Integrated Marketing for Modern Life & Devices, Microsoft, said at CES 2019. "It is not icing on the cake. You need to create a culture that is curious. The expectation is that people don't use the same playbook. You have to create boundaries and fail fast."

I'll add that despite all the challenges, morphing is invigorating. Ride those winds of change and adapt. You and your customers, not to mention your businesses, will be better for it.

Acknowledgements

My name is the only one that appears on the cover of *The Art of Digital Persuasion* but this book has by no means been a solo effort. The experts who I spoke to were generous with their time and wisdom. Mario Schulzke supports me in every thing that I do. Longtime colleague and friend Ed Harrison spent hours away from his family to help polish the manuscript. My wife, family, and friends not yet mentioned were there every step of the way. I thank each one.

The Experts

Lorraine Bardeen

As GM Studio Manager, Mixed Reality, Lorraine Bardeen (@LorraineBardeen) leads Strategy, Production, and Commercial and Media Partnerships for Microsoft HoloLens and several Windows apps and services. She and her team work closely with development studios to craft groundbreaking experiences for Microsoft HoloLens across genres and audiences and to build a rich content portfolio that will inspire creativity and innovation in the new medium.

Bardeen also helps set the long-term strategic roadmap for Microsoft HoloLens as well as Windows apps and experiences across devices, both created by Microsoft and by partners across industries.

Previously, Bardeen led the Microsoft IoT (Internet of Things) Business Group for Europe, Middle East, and Africa, during which time she drove business strategy, partnerships, marketing, and distribution channels.

Scott Emmons

For nearly seven years, Scott Emmons (@scottaemmons) was focused on innovation for the Neiman Marcus Group (NMG). He founded and built the innovation lab (iLab) in

2012. Scott elevated technology innovation to be a core value at the Neiman Marcus Group through his efforts. Until leaving in early 2019 to be Chief Technology officer at consultancy TheCurrent, Scott was responsible for leading NMG in evaluating, designing, testing and piloting cutting-edge technologies and applications for luxury retail. Scott was also working on BYOD (bring your own device) initiatives, Wi-Fi/LAN/WAN infrastructure, mobility and digital signage initiatives. Innovation projects included the Memomi Memory Mirror, 4K touch table look books, store associate IOT communicators, intelligent mobile phone charging stations, digital directories and new fitting room technology.

Dave Isbitski
Dave Isbitski is the Chief Evangelist for Alexa and Echo at Amazon. He has been a professional speaker, trainer, and evangelist for over a decade. He has taught full-day courses on many topics including Voice Design, Natural Language Understanding, Mobile, and the Cloud. Dave has helped launch numerous technology platforms and devices while at both Microsoft and Amazon. He is an author for LinkedIn and can be found on Twitter as @TheDaveDev as well as the official Amazon Blog.

Thom Kennon
Thom Kennon (@tkennon) has founded or led three interactive agencies and consulting groups over his career, including in his current role at Free Radicals.

In 2011, Thom joined the strategic services leadership team at Y&R to lead the creation of the next generation of integrated brand marketing. He guided the transformation of agency thinking and doing around an obsessively behavioral and audience-centric planning model, introducing and evangelizing new tools and practices for briefing, optimization and driving the agency's roster of top tier brand's business results thru freshly integrated marketing.

For the Wunderman global network from 2007-2011, Thom was SVP of Strategy and led a global insights generation practice grounded in applied listening.

Since 2009, he has been teaching Digital Marketing, Social Media and the Brand and Competitive Strategy as adjunct professor at NYU's Master of Science Integrated Marketing program.

Sheryl Kingstone

Sheryl Kingstone (@skingstone) leads 451 Research's coverage for Customer Experience & Commerce, which covers the many aspects of how customer experience is a catalyst for digital transformation. As Vice President, she oversees the company's coverage of a variety of customer experience software markets spanning ad tech, marketing, sales, commerce and service.

Sheryl is a recognized thought leader with over 25 years of experience in the customer experience technologies. She was awarded the CRM Influential Leaders Award and was also the first female to be inducted in the CRM Hall of Fame. Sheryl has extensive speaking experience at conferences and seminars, is quoted in many business and industry journals, and provides consulting expertise to Fortune 1000 companies.

Laura Marriott
Laura Marriott (@kanadawomaninus) has been named one of the industry's 32 Most Powerful Women in Mobile Advertising by Business Insider, Mobile Women to Watch by Mobile Marketer, Top 50 U.S. Executives & Top 50 Women in Mobile Content by Mobile Entertainment and Top 10 Women in Wireless by FierceMarkets. She has led companies and led industries. Laura most recently served as a strategy consultant to mobile tech companies and prior was the Chief Executive Officer and Board Chairperson of NeoMedia, a public small cap company in the mobile ecosystem.

Laura was also global President of the Mobile Marketing Association, the world's leading non-profit trade association for mobile marketing, where she played a critical role in building the organization and the industry from inception. She has over 20 years of experience in leadership, marketing, product and business development in the tech sector.

Tamara McCleary
At the intersection of marketing and technology, Tamara McCleary (@TamaraMcCleary) is an internationally recognized expert on branding, influence and social business. The Founder and CEO of Thulium, a brand amplification company, specializing in B2B social media account-based

marketing, Tamara has expertise is in B2B and B2C marketing, social influence and technology.

Stacy Minero
Stacy Minero (@sminero) is a seasoned strategist with years of experience helping clients develop best in class work and maximize their efforts in marketing and communication. Stacy helps brands elevate their content marketing on Twitter, build creative ideas that earn attention, and adapt video assets for the feed.

She previously led the content strategy practice at Mindshare where she was focused on creating a systematic approach to content from development to discovery and paid distribution.

From 2007-2012, Stacy led Communication Planning for American Express' brand efforts with a focus on insights and creative media ideas. During that time, she helped drive dozens of custom content programs with a slate of cross platform partners. These include NBC, ABC, FOX, Bravo, Conde Nast Entertainment, Hearst Digital, Amazon, Apple, Twitter, YouTube and Roku. Earlier in her career Stacy worked as a Strategic Planner on P&G, Coca-Cola and Hershey accounts.

Aaron Price
Aaron Price is Chief Marketing Officer for Brand Expedia Group, managing global online and customer marketing, strategic distribution partnerships (co-branded and white labeled) and SEM for a variety of the company's travel

brands. Price has been with Expedia for over 14 years, and is a seasoned technology professional who brings critical test-and-learn insight to the evolving marketing industry.

Ben Reubenstein
Currently serving as CEO of POSSIBLE Mobile, Ben Reubenstein (@benr75) brings years of experience in mobile development & strategy, starting with one of the first 150 apps in both the iOS App Store and the Google Play Store. He leads an elite team of mobile-centric professionals to delight customers. Ben's experience as a systems architect allows him to work with customers to deliver solutions that balance technology and business objectives.

Jason Spero
Jason Spero (@Speroman) serves as Vice President, Performance Media, at Google. He was previously the Head of Global Mobile Sales and Strategy. He is responsible for the global priorities and overall commercial strategy for Google's mobile offerings including Search, GDN, AdMob, YouTube and DoubleClick Platforms.

Ryan Spoon
As Senior Vice President of Digital & Social, Ryan Spoon (@ryanspoon) oversees ESPN's digital video and off-platform content, strategy, and execution. From delivering real-time highlights and news to creating platform-exclusive shows like SportsCenter on Snapchat, #RankingsReactions on Twitter, and First Take: Your Take on Facebook Watch,

ESPN social has nearly 300 million followers (Facebook, Instagram, Snapchat, Twitter, YouTube, etc) and drives billions of monthly interactions.

Spoon joined ESPN in July 2012 and led ESPN's digital product, design and audience development teams — responsible for ESPN's digital experience across ESPN.com, mobile apps, fantasy games and OTT experiences. Each month, those properties reach over 125 million unique users — making ESPN the #1 digital sports property both in the U.S. and globally.

The Author

Jeff Hasen

Jeff Hasen (@jeffhasen) enables brands to get closer to their customers in times upended by new devices and behaviors. The results are increased sales and loyalty and businesses doing the disrupting rather than being disrupted.

Over the last decade, he has become one the leading marketers, strategists, and voices in mobile and emerging technology.

Jeff has spoken across the world more than 200 times on his core belief that everything and nothing has changed – marketers still need to sell more stuff and it is simply the how that is different.

A two-time agency president, Jeff is the author of three books – *The Art of Digital Persuasion, The Art of Mobile Persuasion,* and *Mobilized Marketing: Driving Sales, Engagement, and Loyalty Through Mobile Devices.*

As Chief Marketing Officer, he drove mobile marketing company Hipcricket's annual revenue 25X, and helped lead the company to a public market listing, to designation by CTIA as a pioneer and by a leading wireless analyst as an "industry powerhouse", and through its eventual acquisition in 2011.

www.ingramcontent.com/pod-product-compliance
Lightning Source LLC
Chambersburg PA
CBHW030650220526
45463CB00005B/1721